The Complete Instant Pot Cookbook with Healthy Rec Beginn

By Joanna Barton

Contents

What is Instant Pot?

I think everybody has heard about Instant Pot. It is a multi-use kitchen gadget that is used as a steamer, yogurt maker, slow cooker, rice maker, pressure cooker etc. It is replacing all necessary kitchen appliances. All in one! It is also saving money and time. Instant Pot has programs, which are specifically designed to make your perfect meal. Your Instant Pot includes a cooker base with the control panel and heating element; a removable inner pot; a lid with a gasket and valve and other accessories such as trivet, steaming basket, racks, measuring cups and other.

How does the Instant Pot work?

It helps food to cook faster by utilizing the power of hot, trapped steam. This steam helps force the liquid and moisture into the food so dry beans, grains and tough meats get very tender for a short time. It is time to start using your Instant Pot. Here are three main steps:

Step 1: Place ingredients in a removable inner pot. Be careful not to exceed the maximum level (marked on the pot). Store all ingredients in the inner pot to prevent contact from heating elements.

Step 2: Seal the lid and press the desired button. After a few seconds the cooking cycle will start automatically. You should turn the steam release knob to the sealed position.

Step 3: When the Instant Pot complete cooking cycle, release the pressure and remove the lid carefully.

Instant Pot Cooking Programs?

STEAM - This program is good for steaming fish, vegetables and selfish. You should use a steamer basket or metal trivet. If you want to steam vegetables use the Less mode, for fish use the Normal mode and for meat- More mode.

BEAN/ CHILI - With this program you can cook beans for less time. Almost all beans take up to 30 minutes to cook. Use for very soft beans- More mode program, for softer beans- Normal mode and for firm texture beans, use the Less mode.

MANUAL - This is my favorite setting, you can control very easily the temperature and cooking time.

RICE - For Basmati rice, cook time is 4-7 minutes, Jasmine rice takes 3-4 minutes, Brown rice takes 22- 27 minutes and Wild rice will require 25-29 minutes. Before pressure cooking, rinse your rise and you should measure a 1:1 ratio of water-to-rice.

SOUP/BROTH - It is the best program for meaty and veggie soups, broths and creamy chowders.

SAUTE - Instead of using a pan you can saute food in your Instant Pot. You can use for thickening, simmering, searing or browning.

POULTRY - Small portions of chicken will take up to 15 minutes, large pieces of poultry will take 25 minutes and frozen chicken will require around 35 minutes.

KEEP WARM / CANCEL - When your Instant Pot completes its cooking cycle, you should press the "Cancel" button. If you don't do that the "Keep Warm" function will be activated automatically to keep food warm.

MEAT/STEW - This is a good setting for cooking meat. For softer texture use - Less mode and for very tender meat use- More mode.

PORRIDGE - It is good for making oatmeal and rice porridge (congee). Use natural pressure release with this function.

SLOW COOK - You can change the cooking time by using the "+/-" button. You can select also the cooking duration (30 minutes to 20 hours) or a cooking mode (Normal, More and Less).

MULTIGRAIN - This program is good for whole grains, cereal, white rice and brown rice.

EGGS - Good setting for cooking eggs. You can select from Less, Normal or More mode, depending on the egg softness or hardness.

YOGURT - Make homemade yogurt effortless with this two- step program. For yogurt beginner, you can use 1 tablespoon of prepared yogurt for every quart milk.

NATURAL RELEASE and QUICK RELEASE – There are two ways to release the pressure: Press the "Cancel" button to perform a natural pressure release and quick release- manually release the steam

Benefits of the Instant Pot

Here are 5 important benefits of your Instant Pot:

Extremely safe to use- Instant Pot has many safety mechanisms and technologies. So, don't be afraid to use it.

Very healthy and tasty food- since the food is cooked less time, there are remaining more nutrients, which means that the food is much healthy and delicious.

You can cook meals faster- the best thing about Instant Pot is that it will save you cooking time and will spend less energy apart from other cooking methods.

Super simple and easy to use - you just need to know a few buttons and follow some simple instructions. Mostly I use only four buttons: "Manual", "Saute", "+" and "-".

Cooking without smell, sweat, steam, and noise - While cooking you will not feel like you are in the sauna and Instant Pot gives you total piece in your kitchen.

Cool Tips for Your Instant Pot

- **First, read the manufacturer's instructions before using a new device** - Be patient to read all the directions and then enjoy your cooking.
- **Don't forget to use liquid while cooking** - your Pressure cooker builds pressure by using steam. The liquid creates the steam pressure that cooks your food faster. The minimum amount of liquid that your pressure cooker requires is ½ cup (it can be water, broth, wine, tomato juice or fruit juice). You can always use a thickener such as arrowroot powder, all-purpose flours, cornstarch after pressure cooking. Only press the "Sauté" function and let the cooking liquid simmer until your desired consistency.
- **Never force a pressure lid open** - Always release any remaining pressure before removing the cooker's lid. The float valve will drop down and you can safely remove the cooker's lid.
- **Don't mix foods at the same time** - all ingredients have different cook times. That's why you should cook them in phases.
- **Don't worry if you make mistakes** - mistakes are part of the learning process. Never stop to experiment.
- **Regulate the temperature** - you can regulate the temperature while using "Slow cooker" or "Saute" function. It will make it easier to get the perfect cooking temperature.
- **Get an additional sealing ring** - you should have one additional ring for sweet foods and another for savory meals. It is necessary because sealing rings hold onto smell of previous dishes.
- **Always have a thickener in your kitchen** - Instant Pot retains liquid. When you have a dish with extra liquid, just use cornstarch mixed with water.
- **You can use the dishwasher for your Instant pot** - inner pot, steamer rack and other Instant Pot accessories can be washed in the dishwasher. Only the outside of the Instant Pot should

be cleaned with a wet towel.

- **Stock your cupboard with important foods** - I will give you a basic list but it can vary depending on the type of diet you are following:
  1. **Legumes** - rice, beans, lentils, and peas.
  2. **Nuts-** walnuts, almonds, etc.
  3. **Stocks and canned goods** - they include tomato juice, pumpkin purée, pasta sauce, chicken broth, vegetable broth, etc.
  4. **Onion, garlic and shallot** - they add flavor to your dish
  5. **Oils, vinegar, herbs, and spices -** are make cooking at home very easy.
  6. **Frozen items** - fruits, vegetables, fresh or precooked meats can be your best friends when you get home late. Just remember that frozen meats require 50% more of the recommended cooking time. You can follow cooking time tables

Questions and Answers

Here I will share with you the answers of the most asked questions:

- **What release should I use- natural or quick?**
  Most of the recipes contain instructions on which release to use. Choose natural release when you are cooking meat, eggs, vegetables, rice, soup or mostly liquid meals.

- **What size Instant Pot I should purchase?**
  Let me explain to you – 5-Quart IP can feed up to 5 people, and an 8-Quart IP can feed up to 8 people, and so forth. If you have doubts purchase a bigger model.

- **If I double a recipe, do I need to double the cooking time?**
  It is not necessary to double the cooking time. Keep in mind that a larger amount of food does not mean longer cook times. Instant Pot cooks everything at the same rate.

- **Can I use multiple buttons while cooking?**
  Of course, you can use multiple buttons. While cooking you may start with the "Saute" button, then you can press the "Manual" button and when the food is cooked you can use

the "Keep Warm" function.

- **How I can clean my Instant Pot?**
  After each use, you should wash the inner pot. Using a dishcloth, carefully wipe it down. Then you should wash your silicone ring on the inside of the Instant Pot. The last thing is to clean the inside of the lid.

- **What types of accessories I should buy?**
  My top accessories are glass lid, steamer basket, cupcake silicon liners, cake pan, egg steamer rack, gripper clips, and silicone lid.

- **"Burn" message, what does it mean?**
  First - Don't panic! This thing happens when there is not enough liquid in the inner pot. Press the "Cancel" button and move the pressure release to "Vent". Then clean the bottom of the pot with a wooden spoon and stir in any type of liquid (at least ½ cup).

- **Why Instant Pot needs more time to release the pressure?**
  When there are more ingredients in the Instant Pot, it will take more time to build pressure and don't forget to seal the lid.

- **Should I worry when my Instant Pot is making clicking sounds?**
  There are two causes for clicking noises: First cause- probably your inner pot is wet on the outside. The second cause - when Instant Pot is regulating power. This is normal, don't get stressed!

- **"PIP" cooking, what does it mean?**
  "PIP" means pot-in-pot cooking. It is a method for cooking in layers, using a trivet. This method is used when you don't want to cook in the liquid.

CHICKEN

Juicy Chicken with Rice and Mushrooms

Ingredients

- 1 large yellow onion, chopped
- 2 garlic cloves, sliced
- 1 teaspoon dried rosemary
- 2 chicken breasts, boneless
- 1 cup white rice
- 2 tablespoons olive oil
- 1 ½ cup brown mushrooms, sliced
- 2 cups vegetable broth
- 2 carrots, chopped
- 1 teaspoon dried oregano
- salt and pepper, to taste
- ½ cup fresh parsley, chopped

Nutritional Information

402 Calories
13.8g Fat
32.2g Carbs
2.4g Fiber
23g Protein

Directions

Preheat your Instant Pot by pressing the "Sauté" button and heat the olive oil. Season the chicken breasts with salt and pepper.

Sear the chicken breasts for 2 minutes on each side. Stir in the garlic, onion, carrot, mushrooms, rice and vegetable broth. Season with dried rosemary, salt, pepper and oregano. Mix well.

Secure the lid. Choose the "Manual" mode and cook for 12 minutes at High pressure. When cooking is complete, use a quick pressure release and carefully remove the lid.

Serve warm and sprinkle with fresh parsley.

Papa's Chicken Thighs with Potatoes

(Ready in about 20 minutes | Servings 4)

Ingredients

- 2 tablespoons vegetable oil
- 1 lb chicken thighs
- 1 large onion, sliced
- 1 ½ lb red potatoes, peeled and diced
- 2 cloves garlic, sliced
- 1 teaspoon red pepper flakes
- salt and pepper, to taste
- 1 teaspoon dried basil
- 1 teaspoon dried rosemary
- 1 ½ cups chicken broth
- ½ cup parmesan cheese, grated

Nutritional Information

375 Calories
18.9g Fat
27.2g Carbs
.1g Fiber
24.6g Protein

Directions

Preheat your Instant Pot by pressing the "Sauté" button and heat the vegetable oil. Season the chicken thighs with salt, red pepper flakes and pepper.

Sear the chicken thighs for 3 minutes on each side. Set aside.

With wooden spoon clean the brown bits from the pot. Then add the chicken broth to the pot. Stir in the red potatoes, garlic and chicken thighs. Season with dried rosemary, salt, pepper and basil. Mix well.

Secure the lid. Choose the "Manual" mode and cook for 10 minutes at High pressure. When cooking is complete, use a quick pressure release and carefully remove the lid.

Serve warm and sprinkle with parmesan cheese.

Incredible Chicken Thighs in Tomato Sauce

(Ready in about 20 minutes | Servings 4)

Ingredients

- 4 chicken thighs, skinless
- 2 tablespoons butter
- 1 large onion, diced
- 1 cup red bell pepper, diced
- 2 cups tomato puree
- 4 garlic cloves, halved
- 1/2 teaspoon red pepper flakes
- 1/2 cup chicken broth
- 1 teaspoon paprika
- salt and pepper, to taste
- 1 bay leaf
- 2 tablespoons fresh basil, chopped

Nutritional Information

285 Calories
12.9g Fat
18.9g Carbs
4g Fiber
26.6g Protein

Directions

Preheat your Instant Pot by pressing the "Sauté" button and heat the butter. Season the chicken thighs with salt, red pepper flakes and pepper.

Sear the chicken thighs for 3 minutes on each side. Stir in the garlic, onion, red bell pepper, tomato puree and chicken broth. Season with paprika, salt, pepper and bay leaf. Mix well.

Secure the lid. Choose the "Manual" mode and cook for 10 minutes at High pressure. When cooking is complete, use a quick pressure release and carefully remove the lid.

Serve warm and sprinkle with fresh basil.

Spicy Chicken Wings

(Ready in about 30 minutes | Servings 6)

Ingredients

- 3 pounds chicken wings
- 1 teaspoon salt
- 2 teaspoons garlic powder
- 1 teaspoon flour
- 1 tablespoon BBQ sauce
- 1 tablespoon ketchup
- 5 tablespoons butter
- 1/2 teaspoon pepper
- 1/2 cup chicken broth
- 1/2 cup hot sauce
- 1 tablespoon Maple syrup

Nutritional Information

427 Calories
20.1g Fat
6.9g Carbs
0.4g Fiber
55g Protein

Directions

Preheat your Instant Pot by pressing the "Sauté" button and heat 3 tablespoons of butter. Season the chicken wings with salt, garlic powder and pepper.

Sear the chicken thighs for 3-4 minutes on each side. Stir in the chicken broth and secure the lid.

Choose the "Manual" mode and cook for 10 minutes at High pressure. When cooking is complete, use a quick pressure release and carefully remove the lid.

Remove the chicken wings from the Instant Pot and place them in a large bowl. Set aside.

In another medium bowl mix the the maple syrup, hot sauce, ketchup and BBQ sauce. Pour the half of the sauce over the chicken wings and mix well.

Place the chicken wings on a baking dish covered with a baking sheet and bake them for 3-4 minutes per side or until golden brown.

Serve the chicken wings and top with the remaining sauce.

Veggie Chicken Thighs

(Ready in about 20 minutes | Servings 4)

Ingredients

- 1 red bell pepper, seeded and thinly sliced
- 1 large onion, chopped
- 2 carrots, sliced
- 4 chicken thighs
- 1 bell green pepper, seeded and thinly sliced
- 1 cup vegetable broth
- 1 cup sweet potato, sliced into cubes
- 1 bell yellow pepper, seeded and thinly sliced
- 1 small zucchini, diced
- 4 garlic cloves, sliced
- 1 tablespoon vegetable oil
- ½ teaspoon dried thyme
- ½ teaspoon dried sage
- salt and pepper, to taste
- 2 tablespoons fresh rosemary

Nutritional Information

295 Calories
15.6g Fat
11.9g Carbs
2.4g Fiber
25.5g Protein

Directions

Preheat your Instant Pot by pressing the "Sauté" button and heat the vegetable oil. Season the chicken thighs with salt and pepper.

Sear the chicken thighs for 3 minutes on each side. Stir in the garlic, onion, red bell pepper, carrots, sweet potato, green bell pepper, vegetable broth, yellow bell pepper and zucchini.

Season with the dried sage, salt, pepper and dried thyme. Mix well.

Secure the lid. Choose the "Manual" mode and cook for 8 minutes at High pressure. When cooking is complete, use a quick pressure release and carefully remove the lid.

Serve warm and sprinkle with fresh rosemary.

Juicy Chicken Breasts with Lemon

Ingredients

- 1 lb. chicken breasts
- 1/2 cup chicken broth
- 1/2 teaspoon basil
- 2 tablespoons olive oil
- 1 teaspoon red pepper flakes
- 3 garlic cloves, sliced
- 1/2 teaspoon thyme
- 1/3 cup fresh lemon juice
- 2 tablespoons heavy cream
- 1/3 cup parmesan cheese, grated
- 1/2 teaspoon pepper
- ½ teaspoon salt

Nutritional Information

497 Calories
32.6g Fat
5.9g Carbs
0.4g Fiber
43.3g Protein

Directions

Preheat your Instant Pot by pressing the "Sauté" button and heat the olive oil. Season the chicken breasts with salt and pepper.

Saute the chicken breasts for 2-3 minutes on each side. Stir in the garlic, lemon juice, chicken broth, salt, pepper basil, red pepper flakes and thyme. Mix well.

Secure the lid. Choose the "Manual" mode and cook for 8 minutes at High pressure. When cooking is complete, use a quick pressure release and carefully remove the lid.

Remove the chicken breasts from the instant pot.

Add the parmesan cheese and heavy cream to the cooking liquid and stir. Press the "Sauté" button and let it simmer until it gets thick.

Serve the chicken breasts and top with the sauce.

Divine Roast Chicken

(Ready in about 35 minutes | Servings 5)

Ingredients

- 3 pounds whole chicken
- 3 tablespoons olive oil
- 1 teaspoon onion powder
- 1 ½ teaspoon garlic powder
- 2 teaspoons paprika
- 1 1/2 cup chicken broth
- ½ teaspoon dried oregano
- ½ teaspoon dried thyme
- Salt and pepper, to taste

Nutritional Information

499 Calories
22.8g Fat
3g Carbs
0.7g Fiber
70.3g Protein

Directions

In a small bowl mix the olive oil, garlic powder, salt, pepper, paprika, onion powder, dried oregano and dried thyme.

Pat the chicken dry. Rub the mixture all over the chicken. Place the chicken in the inner pot.

Pour the chicken broth into the inner pot.

Secure the lid. Choose "Manual" mode. Cook for 20 minutes at High pressure. When cooking is complete, use a natural pressure release and carefully remove the lid.

Leave to rest for 10 minutes before slicing.

Cheesy Chicken Breasts

(Ready in about 20 minutes | Servings 3)

Ingredients

- 3 chicken breasts, boneless
- 1/3 cup cheddar cheese, grated
- 1/2 teaspoon dried oregano
- 2 tablespoons olive oil
- 1/2 cup heavy cream
- 1 teaspoon paprika
- 1 teaspoon garlic powder
- salt and pepper, to taste
- ½ cup chicken broth
- 1 teaspoon onion powder
- 1/3 cup parmesan cheese, grated
- 1/3 cup green scallions, diced

Nutritional Information

554 Calories
44g Fat
5.8g Carbs
1g Fiber
60.1g Protein

Directions

Preheat your Instant Pot by pressing the "Sauté" button and heat the olive oil. Season the chicken breasts with salt and pepper.

Saute the chicken breasts for 2-3 minutes on each side. Add the chicken broth, garlic powder, onion powder, salt, pepper, paprika and oregano.

Secure the lid. Choose "Manual" mode and cook for 8 minutes at High pressure. When cooking is complete, use a natural pressure release and carefully remove the lid.

Stir in the parmesan cheese, heavy cream and cheddar cheese.

Cover with the lid, and let it sit in the residual heat for 5 minutes.

Serve immediately and garnish with green scallions.

Super Easy Chicken Sandwiches

(Ready in about 25 minutes | Servings 6)

Ingredients

- 2 pounds, chicken breasts, skinless
- ½ cup vegetable broth
- ½ teaspoon paprika
- 1 teaspoon dried oregano
- 2 garlic cloves, sliced
- 1/3 cup fresh green onions, chopped
- salt and pepper, to taste
- 2 tablespoons butter
- 1/3 cup mustard
- 1/3 cup mayonnaise
- 1 large tomato, sliced
- 6 lettuce leaves
- 6 hamburger buns

Nutritional Information

386 Calories
16.1g Fat
22g Carbs
2.7g Fiber
39.7g Protein

Directions

Preheat your Instant Pot by pressing the "Sauté" button and melt the butter. Season the chicken breasts with salt and pepper.

Saute the chicken breasts for 2-3 minutes on each side. Add the vegetable broth, garlic, paprika and oregano.

Secure the lid. Choose the "Manual" mode and cook for 8 minutes at High pressure. When cooking is complete, use a quick pressure release and carefully remove the lid.

Shred the chicken with two forks.

Spread the mayonnaise on the bottom half of each hamburger bun. Then place the lettuce leaves and top with the shredded chicken, tomato, mustard and green onion. Top with the remaining bun halves and serve.

Parmesan Chicken Meatballs

(Ready in about 15 minutes | Servings 5)

Ingredients

- 1 yellow onion, diced
- 1 ½ cup marinara sauce
- 2 tablespoons olive oil
- 1/3 cup fresh parsley, chopped
- 2 pounds ground chicken
- 1/3 cup parmesan cheese
- salt and pepper, to taste
- 2 small eggs, beaten
- 1/2 cup fine breadcrumbs
- 1/2 cup chicken broth

Nutritional Information

439 Calories
26.7g Fat
8.2g Carbs
1.7g Fiber
41.8g Protein

Directions

In a large bowl combine the ground chicken, onion, fresh parsley, breadcrumbs, salt, pepper and eggs. Mix well.

Scoop from the mixture and shape into 1-inch balls.

Preheat your Instant Pot by pressing the "Sauté" button and heat the olive oil. Sear the meatballs until golden brown on all sides. Work in batches and remove from the pot.

Add the marinara sauce and chicken broth in the pot and place back the meatballs.

Secure the lid. Choose the "Manual" mode and cook for 5 minutes at High pressure. When cooking is complete, use a quick pressure release and carefully remove the lid.

Serve immediately.

BEEF

Roasted Beef with Potatoes

Ingredients

- 1 ½ pounds potatoes, cut into large chunks
- 2 ½ pounds beef chuck roast
- 1 tablespoon olive oil
- 1 teaspoon red pepper
- 1 teaspoon dried basil
- 5 cloves garlic, peeled and halved
- 3 cups vegetable broth
- 2 yellow onions, sliced
- salt and pepper, to taste

Nutritional Information

469 Calories
19.3g Fat
22.2g Carbs
2.7g Fiber
51.8g Protein

Directions

Preheat your Instant Pot by pressing the "Sauté" button and heat the olive oil. Season the beef roast with salt and pepper.

Sear the beef roast for 4 minutes on each side. Stir in the potatoes, garlic, onion and vegetable broth.

Season with dried basil, salt, pepper and red pepper and rosemary. Mix well.

Secure the lid. Choose the "Manual" mode and cook for 50 minutes at High pressure. When cooking is complete, use a quick pressure release for 15 minutes and carefully remove the lid.

Slice the beef roast and serve with the potatoes. Enjoy!

Instant Beef Sirloin with Mushrooms

(Ready in about 40 minutes | Servings 3)

Ingredients

- 1 teaspoon smoked paprika
- 1 lb. beef sirloin, cut into cubes
- 1 teaspoon dried basil
- 2 tablespoons butter
- 1/2 teaspoon dried marjoram
- 4 cloves garlic, peeled and halved
- 2 cups beef broth
- 1 lb. button mushrooms, quartered
- 1 shallot, diced
- Salt and pepper, to taste
- 2 tablespoons all-purpose flour

Nutritional Information

421 Calories
25.6g Fat
12.3g Carbs
2.4g Fiber
37.1g Protein

Directions

In a small bowl, combine the flour, salt, pepper, smoked paprika, and marjoram. Dredge the beef cubes in the seasoned mixture. Coat on all sides.

Preheat your Instant Pot by pressing the "Sauté" button and melt the butter. Cook the beef for 4-5 minutes. Then stir in the beef broth and basil.

Secure the lid. Choose the "Meat/Stew" mode and cook for 25 minutes at High pressure. When cooking is complete, use a quick pressure release and carefully remove the lid.

Add in the garlic, quartered mushrooms and shallot.

Secure the lid. Choose the "Manual" mode and cook for 2 minutes at High pressure. When cooking is complete, use a quick pressure release and carefully remove the lid.

Serve warm. Bon appetite!

Tender Beef Stew with Sweet Potatoes

Ingredients

- 1 pound beef round roast, cut into cubes
- 1 teaspoon thyme
- 1 celery, diced
- 1 teaspoon rosemary
- 2 tablespoons olive oil
- 3 cups vegetable broth
- 1 ½ tablespoon tomato paste
- 1 large sweet onion, chopped
- 2 medium sweet potatoes, peeled and cut into cubes
- 2 carrots, sliced into circles
- Salt and pepper, to taste
- 1 bay leaf
- 1/3 cup fresh parsley, chopped

Directions

Preheat your Instant Pot by pressing the "Sauté" button and heat the olive oil. Cook the beef for 4-5 minutes. Then stir in the onion, celery and carrot. Saute for 2-3 minutes.

Add in the tomato paste, sweet potatoes and vegetable broth. Season with bay leaf, salt, pepper, rosemary and thyme. Stir well.

Secure the lid. Choose the "Manual" mode and cook for 20 minutes at High pressure. When cooking is complete, use a quick pressure release and carefully remove the lid.

Serve and sprinkle with fresh parsley. Enjoy!

Nutritional Information

354 Calories
17.1g Fat
24g Carbs
3.4g Fiber
35.4g Protein

Mexican Ground Beef Bowl

(Ready in about 20 minutes | Servings 4)

Ingredients

- 1 cup vegetable broth
- ½ red onion chopped
- 1 can black beans, drained and rinsed
- 1 teaspoon chili powder
- 2 teaspoons smoked paprika
- 2 garlic cloves, minced
- ½ teaspoon dried cumin
- ½ teaspoon dried oregano
- 1 red bell pepper, deseeded and sliced
- 1 can diced tomatoes
- ½ cup frozen corn
- 1 pound ground beef
- 1 cup cheddar cheese, shredded
- 1 tablespoon olive oil
- Salt and pepper, to taste

Nutritional Information

324 Calories
19.8g Fat
10.2g Carbs
2.5g Fiber
32.1g Protein

Directions

Press the "Sauté" button to preheat your Instant Pot. Heat the olive oil and cook the ground beef for 3 minutes.

Then stir in the red bell pepper, vegetable broth, red onion, corn, tomatoes, and black beans. Season with chili powder, smoked paprika, salt, pepper, cumin, and oregano.

Secure the lid. Choose the "Manual" mode and cook for 8 minutes at High pressure. When cooking is complete, use a natural pressure release and carefully remove the lid.

Serve into bowls and top with the shredded cheddar cheese. Bon appetite!

Traditional Beef Short Ribs

(Ready in about 1 hour | Servings 4)

Ingredients

- 2 pounds beef short ribs, bone-in
- 2 tablespoons olive oil
- 3 tablespoons brown sugar
- 2 teaspoon smoked paprika
- 1 ½ teaspoon garlic powder
- 1 ½ teaspoon onion powder
- 1 cup water
- 1 ½ teaspoon Kosher salt
- 1 teaspoon pepper
- 1/3 teaspoon cinnamon

Nutritional Information

463 Calories
27.3g Fat
9.1g Carbs
0.9g Fiber
46.3g Protein

Directions

Mix all Ingredients into a bowl. Rub the mixture on both sides of the ribs.

Place the water and a metal trivet into the Instant Pot.

Secure the lid. Choose the "Manual" mode and cook for 45 minutes at High pressure. When cooking is complete, use a natural pressure release for 5 minutes and carefully remove the lid.

Then place the short ribs under the broiler until crispy for 7-8 minutes.

Serve with your favorite barbecue sauce and enjoy!

Aromatic Salad with Beef

Ingredients

- 1 pound beef steak
- Salt and pepper, to taste
- 1 cucumber, sliced
- 1 large red onion, diced
- 1/2 teaspoon red pepper flakes
- 1 cup water
- 1/4 cup olive oil, divided
- 2 tablespoons wine vinegar
- 1 tablespoon lime juice
- 1 teaspoon sugar
- 1 ½ tablespoon fresh cilantro, finely chopped
- 1 ½ large tomatoes, cut into cubes
- 3 cups green salad mix
- 1/2 cup feta cheese, crumbled
- 1 tablespoon sesame seeds

Nutritional Information

384 Calories
25.9g Fat
10.6g Carbs
2.9g Fiber
28.8g Protein

Directions

Season the steak with salt and pepper. Then add the steak, water and red pepper flakes to the inner pot

Secure the lid. Choose the "Manual" mode and cook for 25 minutes at High pressure. When cooking is complete, use a natural pressure release for 5 minutes and carefully remove the lid.

Slice the steak into thin strips and transfer to the salad bowl. Stir in the tomatoes, cucumber, green salad mix, fresh cilantro, and crumbled feta cheese. Combine well.

In a small bowl add the lime juice, wine vinegar, olive oil and sugar. Stir. Drizzle the prepared dressing over the salad and mix.

Sprinkle with sesame seeds and serve. Bon appetite!

Simple Stuffed Peppers with Beef

Ingredients

- 6 large green bell peppers, washed, de-seeded and cored
- 1 yellow onion, chopped
- 2 garlic cloves, minced
- 2 carrots, finely chopped
- Salt and pepper, to taste
- 2 teaspoons marjoram
- 2/3 cup cooked rice
- 1 teaspoon basil
- 2 tablespoons fresh parsley, chopped
- 2 tablespoons breadcrumbs
- 1 ½ cup tomato puree
- 1 ½ pound ground beef
- 1 cup parmesan cheese, grated
- 1 cup water

Nutritional Information

486 Calories
28.7g Fat
25.6g Carbs
7.7g Fiber
38.8g Protein

Directions

In a large bowl mix the ground beef, rice, onion, parsley, breadcrumbs, carrots, basil, marjoram, tomato puree, garlic, salt and pepper.

Add 1 cup of water and a metal trivet to the bottom. Fill the pepper with the mixture

Lower the casserole dish onto the trivet in the Instant Pot.

Secure the lid. Choose the "Manual" mode and cook for 9 minutes at High pressure. When cooking is complete, use a natural pressure release for 5 minutes and carefully remove the lid.

Serve and top with parmesan cheese. Enjoy!

Italian Meatballs with Parmesan

Ingredients

- 1 pound ground beef
- 1 yellow onion, diced
- 2 cloves garlic, minced
- 2 small eggs, beaten
- ½ cup breadcrumbs
- 1/3 cup parmesan cheese
- Salt and pepper, to taste
- 1 tablespoon olive oil
- 1 ½ can tomato puree
- 1 can crushed tomatoes
- 1 cup vegetable broth
- 1 teaspoon sugar
- 2 teaspoons dried basil

Nutritional Information

472 Calories
20.9g Fat
33.3g Carbs
7.1g Fiber
40.7g Protein

Directions

In a large bowl mix the ground beef, eggs, garlic, yellow onion, breadcrumbs, parmesan, salt and pepper.

Shape the mixture into 1-inch meatballs. Then press the "Sauté" button and heat the olive oil. Saute the meatballs for 5-6 minutes.

Pour over them the tomato puree, basil, sugar, broth and crushed tomatoes.

Secure the lid. Choose the "Manual" mode and cook for 12 minutes at High pressure. When cooking is complete, use a natural pressure release for 10 minutes and carefully remove the lid.

Serve warm. Bon appétit!

Winter Beef Soup

Ingredients

- 2 tablespoons vegetable oil
- 1 pound beef chuck, cut into cubes
- Salt and pepper, to taste
- 4 cups beef broth
- 2 teaspoons dried oregano
- 2 large carrots, diced
- 1 small leek, sliced
- 2 cloves garlic, sliced
- 1/2 cup frozen corn
- 1 cup frozen peas
- ½ cup frozen green beans
- 1 medium potato, cut into small cubes
- 1 large red bell pepper, chopped

Nutritional Information

367 Calories
13.4g Fat
34.3g Carbs
7.1g Fiber
28.3g Protein

Directions

Press the "Sauté" button to preheat your Instant Pot. Heat the vegetable oil and add the beef cubes. Cook for 3 minutes.

Then add the leek, carrots and garlic. Saute for 1-2 minutes. Stir in the beef broth, frozen corn, green beans, peas, red bell pepper and potato. Season with salt, pepper and oregano.

Secure the lid. Choose the "Manual" mode and cook for 9 minutes at High pressure. When cooking is complete, use a quick pressure release for 15minutes and carefully remove the lid.

Serve warm. Bon appetite!

Filet Mignon with Wild Mushrooms

Ingredients

- 1 pound filet mignon, about 1 ½-inch thick
- 1 ½ cup cream of onion soup
- Salt and pepper, to taste
- 2 tablespoons butter
- 2 large onions, sliced into circles
- 2 garlic cloves, sliced
- 1/3 cup heavy cream
- 1 teaspoon tarragon
- 3 tablespoons, all-purpose flour

Nutritional Information

446 Calories
22.5g Fat
24.3g Carbs
2.7g Fiber
38.2g Protein

Directions

Season the filet mignon with salt, flour and pepper.

Press the "Sauté" button and melt the butter. Cook for 1-2 minutes per side.

Add in the onion and garlic, saute for 1 minute. Stir in the cream of onion soup, salt, pepper, and tarragon.

Choose the "Meat/Stew" mode and cook for 15 minutes at High Pressure. When cooking is complete, use a quick pressure release and carefully remove the lid.

Stir in the heavy cream and press the "Sauté" button one more time. Boil for 3-4 minutes more.

Serve immediately and enjoy!

PORK

Parmesan Pork Loin with Russet Potatoes

Ingredients

- 1 pound russet potatoes, peeled and diced into cubes
- 1 ½ teaspoon red pepper flakes
- 1 teaspoon dried thyme
- 4 tablespoons parmesan cheese, grated
- 1 teaspoon dried thyme
- 1 ½ pound pork loin
- 3 cloves garlic, sliced
- 2 cups vegetable broth
- salt and pepper, to taste
- 1 teaspoon onion powder
- 1 teaspoon dried parsley
- 3 tablespoons olive oil

Nutritional Information

463 Calories
24.2g Fat
21g Carbs
1.7g Fiber
38.7g Protein

Directions

Preheat your Instant Pot by pressing the "Sauté" button. Season the pork loin with salt and pepper. Then heat the olive oil and sear the pork loin for 6-7 minutes per side.

When the pork is seared on each side, press the "Cancel" button and remove it from the instant pot and place the pork on the cooking board and cut into slices.

If there are any brown bits clean them with a wooden spoon.

Put back in the instant pot the sliced pork, russet potatoes and garlic. Season with salt, pepper, red pepper flakes, onion powder, dried parsley and dried thyme.

Pour in the vegetable stock and secure the lid. Choose the "Manual" mode and High pressure; cook for 15 minutes. When cooking is complete, use a quick pressure release and carefully remove the lid.

Serve and top with parmesan cheese.

Amazing Pork Chops with Apple Sauce

(Ready in about 20 minutes | Servings 3)

Ingredients

- 2 large apples, cored and sliced
- 1 yellow onion, sliced
- 1 teaspoon garlic powder
- 3 pork chops
- Kosher salt and pepper, to taste
- 1 teaspoon dried rosemary
- 2 tablespoons butter
- 1/2 cup apple juice
- 2 tablespoons fresh parsley, chopped

Nutritional Information

463 Calories
25.4g Fat
27.6g Carbs
4.2g Fiber
41.2g Protein

Directions

Preheat your Instant Pot by pressing the "Sauté" button and melt the butter. Season the pork chops with garlic powder, salt and pepper.

Sear the pork chops for 2 minutes per side. Stir in the yellow onion, sliced apples and apple juice.

Season with salt, pepper, rosemary and parsley. Stir well.

Secure the lid. Choose the "Manual/Pressure cook" mode and cook for 10 minutes at High pressure. When cooking is complete, use a quick pressure release and carefully remove the lid.

Serve immediately. Bon appetite!

Juicy Pork Meatballs

(Ready in about 20 minutes | Servings 4)

Ingredients

- 1 cup vegetable broth
- ½ teaspoon onion powder
- 1 pounds ground pork
- 2 tablespoons olive oil
- ½ cup bread crumbs
- 1 teaspoon red pepper flakes
- 1 teaspoon salt
- 2 tablespoons fresh parsley, chopped
- 1 teaspoon pepper
- 2 eggs
- 1/3 cup Parmesan cheese, grated

Nutritional Information

517 Calories
37.6g Fat
0.4g Carbs
4.2g Fiber
36.7g Protein

Directions

In a large bowl combine the ground pork, onion powder, bread crumbs, eggs, Parmesan cheese and fresh parsley. Season with salt, pepper and red pepper flakes.

Mix well and form into small meatballs.

Press the "Sauté" button and heat the olive oil. Sear your meatballs until golden brown on all sides. Work in batches.

Serve warm with your favorite salad.

Tender Pork Baby Ribs

(Ready in about 30 minutes | Servings 5)

Ingredients

- 1 tablespoon honey
- 1/2 cup vegetable stock
- 1 ½ teaspoon salt
- 1 teaspoon pepper
- ½ teaspoon chili powder
- 1 teaspoon garlic powder
- 1 rack baby back ribs
- 1/3 cup soy sauce
- 1/2 teaspoon red pepper
- 1 teaspoon dried oregano

Nutritional Information

630 Calories
49.2g Fat
5.8g Carbs
0.4g Fiber
61.3g Protein

Directions

Remove the membrane of the back of the ribs. In a medium bowl mix the honey, salt, pepper, garlic powder, chili powder, soy sauce, red pepper and oregano.

Rub the mixture over both sides of the baby ribs. Add the vegetable stock and secure the lid.

Choose the "Meat/Stew" mode and cook for 20 minutes at High pressure. When cooking is complete, use a quick pressure release and carefully remove the lid.

Serve the pork ribs with your favorite BBQ sauce and enjoy!

Easy Pork Chops with Rice

(Ready in about 20 minutes | Servings 3)

Ingredients

- 3 boneless pork chops
- 1 1/2 cup jasmine rice
- 4 garlic cloves, diced
- 2 tablespoons butter
- 1 yellow onion, sliced
- 1 teaspoon paprika
- 1 can tomatoes, diced
- 1/2 teaspoon cumin
- salt and pepper, to taste
- 1 cup vegetable broth
- 1/3 cup fresh parsley

Nutritional Information

457 Calories
22.7g Fat
25.8g Carbs
9.6g Fiber
48g Protein

Directions

Preheat your Instant Pot by pressing the "Sauté" button and melt the butter. Season the pork chops with salt and pepper.

Sear the pork chops for 3 minutes per side. Stir in the jasmine rice, onion, garlic, diced tomatoes and vegetable broth.

Season with salt, pepper, paprika and cumin. Mix well.

Secure the lid. Choose the "Manual" mode and cook for 10 minutes at High pressure. When cooking is complete, use a quick pressure release and carefully remove the lid.

Serve the pork chops and sprinkle with fresh parsley. Enjoy!

Simple Pork Stew

Ingredients

- 1 ½ lb. pork shoulder
- 1 large onion, chopped
- 4 garlic cloves, sliced
- Kosher salt and pepper, to taste
- 1 teaspoon paprika
- 2 cups baby carrots, washed and trimmed
- 2 celery sticks, diced
- 1 ½ cup chicken broth
- 1 teaspoon thyme
- 2 tablespoons olive oil
- 2 red bell peppers, sliced into strips
- 2 tablespoons sesame seeds, chopped

Nutritional Information

388 Calories
19.8g Fat
11.3g Carbs
2.4g Fiber
41.3g Protein

Directions

Slice the pork shoulder into 2- inch cubes.

Preheat your Instant Pot by pressing the "Sauté" button and heat the olive oil. Season the pork cubes with salt and pepper.

Sear the pork cubes for 2 minutes per side. Stir in the chopped onion, garlic, baby carrots, celery, sliced red bell peppers and chicken broth.

Season with salt, pepper, thyme and paprika. Mix well.

Secure the lid. Choose the "Meat/Stew" mode and cook for 20 minutes at High pressure. When cooking is complete, use a quick pressure release and carefully remove the lid.

Serve the pork cubes and sprinkle with sesame seeds. Enjoy!

Pork with Blue Cheese Sauce

(Ready in about 20 minutes | Servings 2)

Ingredients

- 2 tablespoons butter
- 2 boneless pork chops
- salt and pepper, to taste
- 1 shallot, sliced
- 1/3 cup white wine
- 1/2 cup vegetable broth
- ½ cup blue cheese
- 1/3 cup heavy cream
- 1 tablespoon fresh green onion, chopped

Nutritional Information

528 Calories
34.9g Fat
4.2g Carbs
0.5g Fiber
49.8g Protein

Directions

Press the "Sauté" button and heat the butter. Sear the pork chops for 2 minutes per side and set aside.

If necessary, clean the brown bits from the Instant pot with wooden spoon.

Add the shallot, white wine, vegetable broth, and blue cheese. Mix well.

Place back the pork chops in the Instant Pot. Secure the lid. Choose the "Manual" mode and cook for 8 minutes at High pressure. When cooking is complete, use a natural pressure release and carefully remove the lid.

Seal the lid and stir in the heavy cream. Serve the pork chops warm and sprinkle with fresh green onion.

Tender Pork Chops with Mushrooms

(Ready in about 20 minutes | Servings 4)

Ingredients

- 4 pork chops
- 1/2 teaspoon salt
- 1/2 cup sour cream
- ½ teaspoon turmeric
- 1/2 teaspoon pepper
- 2 cups mushrooms, sliced
- 1 teaspoon paprika
- 4 cloves garlic crushed
- 2 tablespoons olive oil
- 1 teaspoon onion powder
- 1 cup vegetable broth
- 1 cup parmesan cheese, grated

Nutritional Information

544 Calories
34.5g Fat
8g Carbs
0.6g Fiber
48.9g Protein

Directions

Preheat your Instant Pot by pressing the "Sauté" button and heat the olive oil. Season the pork chops with onion powder, salt and pepper.

Sear the pork chops for 2 minutes per side. Stir in the mushrooms, sour cream, vegetable broth, garlic, paprika and turmeric. Stir well.

Secure the lid. Choose the "Meat/Stew" mode and cook for 10 minutes at High pressure. When cooking is complete, use a quick pressure release and carefully remove the lid.

Serve warm and sprinkle with parmesan cheese. Enjoy!

Perfect Pork Cutlets in Tomato Sauce

(Ready in about 20 minutes | Servings 4)

Ingredients

- 2 tablespoons ketchup
- 1 cup tomato paste
- 4 pork cutlets
- salt and pepper, to taste
- 2 garlic cloves, chopped
- ½ tablespoon soy sauce
- 2 small yellow onions, chopped
- 2 red bell peppers, sliced
- 2 tablespoons vegetable oil
- 1 cup vegetable broth
- 1 ½ tablespoon Worcestershire sauce

Nutritional Information

492 Calories
25.8g Fat
23g Carbs
4g Fiber
44.3g Protein

Directions

Preheat your Instant Pot by pressing the "Sauté" button and heat the vegetable oil. Sear the pork cutlets for 2 minutes per side. Set aside.

Add in the garlic, onion, and red bell peppers. Saute for 2-3 minutes. Season with salt and pepper. Stir in the ketchup, tomato paste, soy sauce and Worcestershire sauce. Mix well.

Place the pork cutlets back and pour in the vegetable broth and secure the lid.

Choose the "Manual" mode and High pressure; cook for 12 minutes. When cooking is complete, use a quick pressure release and carefully remove the lid.

Serve the pork cutlets and top with the tomato sauce.

Rich Pork Chops with Green Beans

(Ready in about 30 minutes | Servings 4)

Ingredients

- 4 pork chops
- 1 ½ pound green beans, washed and trimmed
- 2 celery stalks, diced
- 1 teaspoon thyme
- 4 cloves garlic, sliced
- Kosher salt and pepper, to taste
- 2 tablespoons butter
- 1 teaspoon dried rosemary
- 1 large onion, chopped
- 1/2 cup cream of vegetable broth
- 1 teaspoon red pepper
- 2 tablespoons fresh rosemary, chopped

Nutritional Information

388 Calories
23.8g Fat
18.5g Carbs
5.8g Fiber
44g Protein

Directions

Preheat your Instant Pot by pressing the "Sauté" button and melt the butter. Season the pork chops with salt and pepper.

Sear the pork chops for 3 minutes per side. Stir in the green beans, celery, garlic, onion and vegetable broth.

Season with salt, pepper, thyme, red pepper and rosemary. Mix well.

Secure the lid. Choose the "Meat/Stew" mode and cook for 17 minutes at High pressure. When cooking is complete, use a quick pressure release and carefully remove the lid.

Serve the pork chops with the green beans and sprinkle with fresh rosemary. Enjoy!

FISH & SEAFOOD

Classic Codfish with Herbs

(Ready in about 10 minutes | Servings 4)

Ingredients

- 4 fresh codfish fillets
- 1/3 cup hot water
- 4 tablespoons butter
- Sea salt and pepper, to taste
- 1/3 teaspoon paprika
- ½ teaspoon oregano
- ½ teaspoon basil
- ½ teaspoon onion powder
- ½ teaspoon garlic powder
- 4 lemon slices
- 2 tablespoons fresh parsley, chopped

Nutritional Information

334 Calories
13.8g Fat
5g Carbs
0.7g Fiber
41.4g Protein

Directions

Add the hot water into the inner pot and put the steamer rack.

Place the codfish fillets on the rack. Season the fillets with oregano, basil, onion powder, paprika, garlic powder, salt, pepper and fresh parsley.

Secure the lid. Choose the "Steam" mode and cook for 3 minutes at Low pressure. When cooking is complete, use a quick pressure release and carefully remove the lid.

Remove the codfish fillets from the inner pot.

Garnish with the lemon slices and your favorite salad. Serve!

King Crabs with Lemon Sauce

Ingredients

- 3 pounds frozen king crab legs
- 1/2 cup water
- 1/2 cup lemon juice
- Sea salt and pepper, to taste
- 5 tablespoons butter
- 1 ½ tablespoon fresh parsley, chopped
- 1/2 tablespoon fresh thyme, chopped

Nutritional Information

312 Calories
11.4g Fat
2.6g Carbs
0.3g Fiber
41g Protein

Directions

Add the frozen king crab legs, water, salt pepper and thyme to the inner pot.

Secure the lid. Choose the "Manual" mode and cook for 3 minutes at High pressure. When cooking is complete, use a quick pressure release and carefully remove the lid.

Meanwhile in a small pan over medium heat, add the butter, salt and pepper. Cook for 2-3 minutes. Transfer the melted butter in a small bowl and stir in the lemon juice and parsley.

Serve the crab legs warm and drizzle with the lemon sauce. Enjoy!

Red Shrimps with Feta Cheese

(Ready in about 10 minutes | Servings 4)

Ingredients

- 1 1/2 lb. raw shrimp, shelled and deveined
- 1 ½ can diced tomatoes
- 1 teaspoon basil
- 1 large onion, chopped
- 2 tablespoons olive oil
- 3 cloves garlic, diced
- 1 teaspoon turmeric
- ½ cup feta cheese, crumbled
- ½ cup vegetable stock
- 1/2 teaspoon dried oregano

Nutritional Information

356 Calories
14.7g Fat
6.3g Carbs
0.7g Fiber
39.4g Protein

Directions

Add the garlic, onion, canned tomatoes, shrimps, olive oil, basil, vegetable stock, turmeric, oregano, and tomatoes to the inner pot.

Secure the lid. Choose the "Manual" mode and cook for 3 minutes at Low pressure. When cooking is complete, use a quick pressure release and carefully remove the lid.

Top with feta cheese and serve.

Colorful Tuna Fillets with Bell Peppers

(Ready in about 10 minutes | Servings 4)

Ingredients

- 1 large yellow bell pepper, sliced into rings
- 2 lbs. tuna filets
- 1 cup water
- 1 large red bell pepper, sliced into rings
- 2 tablespoons butter, melted
- Salt and black pepper, to taste
- 1 large green bell pepper, sliced into rings

Nutritional Information

264 Calories
8g Fat
4.3g Carbs
0.7g Fiber
44.4g Protein

Directions

Put the water in the inner pot and place the steamer rack.

Place the tuna fillets onto the rack. Add the butter, salt, and pepper; and top with the sliced peppers.

Secure the lid. Choose the "Steam" mode and cook for 4 minutes at Low pressure. When cooking is complete, use a quick pressure release and carefully remove the lid.

Serve warm. Bon appetite!

Tender Salmon with Baby Potatoes

(Ready in about 15 minutes | Servings 3)

Ingredients

- 1 lb. salmon fillets
- Sea salt and pepper, to taste
- 1/2 teaaspoon garlic powder
- 1 tablespoon olive oil
- 1 pound baby potatoes, quartered
- 1/2 lemon, cut into wedges
- 1 cup water
- ½ teaspoon thyme
- ½ teaspoon rosemary

Nutritional Information

357 Calories
12.4g Fat
28.5g Carbs
3.7g Fiber
34.8g Protein

Directions

Place the potatoes at the bottom of the inner pot. Add 1 cup of water. Then, add the olive oil, salt and pepper. Place the rack over the potatoes.

Place the salmon fillets on the rack. Season the fillets with garlic powder, salt, pepper, thyme and rosemary.

Secure the lid. Choose the "Steam" mode and cook for 3 minutes at Low pressure. When cooking is complete, use a quick pressure release and carefully remove the lid.

Remove the salmon and the rack from the inner pot. Then continue to cook the potatoes until fork tender.

Garnish with the lemon wedges and serve.

Sole Fillets with Steamed Green Beans

Ingredients

- 2 tablespoons fresh parsley
- Sea salt and pepper, to taste
- 3 cloves garlic, minced
- 4 cups green beans
- 1 teaspoon dried rosemary
- 2 small shallots, quartered
- 1 1/2 lb. sole fillet
- ½ teaspoon dried thyme
- 1 lemon, cut into wedges

Nutritional Information

219 Calories
2.8g Fat
9.4g Carbs
3.3g Fiber
40g Protein

Directions

Season the sole fillets with salt and pepper. Place the sole fillets to the inner pot and secure the lid.

Choose the "Steam" mode and cook for 3 minutes at Low pressure. When cooking is complete, use a quick pressure release and carefully remove the lid. Reserve.

Then, add the garlic, shallot and green beans to the inner pot. Season with salt, pepper, thyme and rosemary.

Secure the lid. Choose the "Steam" mode and cook for 3 minutes at Low pressure. When cooking is complete, use a quick pressure release and carefully remove the lid.

Serve the sole fillets and garnish with the green beans and lemon wedges.

Aromatic Mussels with Saffron

(Ready in about 10 minutes | Servings 4)

Ingredients

- 2 pounds frozen mussels, cleaned and debearded
- Sea salt and black pepper, to taste
- 2 tablespoons butter
- 1 tablespoon fresh thyme, chopped
- 3 cloves garlic, minced
- 2 shallots, diced
- 1 teaspoon dried oregano
- 1 cup white wine
- saffron threads, crushed
- 2 tablespoons fresh parsley, chopped

Nutritional Information

265 Calories
10.9g Fat
11.2g Carbs
0.5g Fiber
27.9g Protein

Directions

Preheat your Instant Pot by pressing the "Sauté" button and melt the butter. Add in the garlic and shallot. Saute until fragrant.

Stir in the wine, mussel and saffron.

Secure the lid. Choose the "Manual" mode and cook for 3 minutes at Low pressure. When cooking is complete, use a quick pressure release and carefully remove the lid.

Transfer the mussels to serving bowls and sprinkle with fresh parsley.

Sea Bass with Onions and Carrots

Ingredients

- 1 tablespoon olive oil
- 3 carrots, cut into circles
- 2 lbs. sea bass
- Sea salt and pepper, to taste
- 1 tablespoon tamari sauce
- 4 cloves garlic, minced
- 3 large onions, cut into circles
- ½ cup white wine
- 1 tablespoon honey
- 1 cup water

Nutritional Information

235 Calories
5.8g Fat
13.4g Carbs
2.2g Fiber
28.9g Protein

Directions

Preheat your Instant Pot by pressing the "Sauté" button and heat the olive oil. Season the sea bass with salt and pepper. Sear the fish for 2 minutes on each side.

Add 1 cup of water and a steamer rack to the bottom of your Instant Pot. Lower the fish onto the rack.

Secure the lid. Choose the "Steam" mode and cook for 10 minutes at Low pressure. When cooking is complete, use a quick pressure release and carefully remove the lid. Reserve.

Then, add the garlic, white wine, honey, tamari sauce onion and carrot to the inner pot. Season with salt and pepper.

Choose the "Saute" mode and cook for 5 minutes. Stir occasionally and simmer until the sauce thickens.

Serve the fish and spoon the sauce over. Enjoy!

Halibut Steaks with Steamed Carrots

(Ready in about 1 hour | Servings 4)

Ingredients

- 1/2 teaspoon red pepper flakes, crushed
- 1 lb. halibut steaks
- 2 tablespoons olive oil
- 2 tablespoons fresh lemon juice
- Sea salt and pepper, to taste
- 5 cups fresh baby carrots
- 2 teaspoons sesame seeds
- 1 cup water
- 1 tablespoon butter, melted
- 2 tablespoons fresh parsley, chopped

Nutritional Information

360 Calories
26.5g Fat
15.1g Carbs
4.3g Fiber
18.4g Protein

Directions

Add 1 cup of water and a steamer rack to the bottom of your Instant Pot.

Cut 4 sheets of aluminum foil. Place the halibut steak in each sheet of foil. Add the olive oil, salt, and black pepper to the top of the fish and close each packet and seal the edges.

Lower the packets onto the rack.

Secure the lid. Choose the "Steam" mode and cook for 3 minutes at Low pressure. When cooking is complete, use a natural pressure release and carefully remove the lid. Reserve.

Then, add the butter carrots to the inner pot. Season with salt, pepper, thyme and rosemary.

Secure the lid. Choose the "Steam" mode and cook for 8 minutes at Low pressure. When cooking is complete, use a quick pressure release and carefully remove the lid.

Transfer the carrots into a large bowl and season them with parsley, lemon juice and sesame seeds.

Serve the halibut steaks and garnish with the carrots.

Sweet Caramel Tilapia Fillets

(Ready in about 15 minutes | Servings 4)

Ingredients

- 4 tilapia fillets, skin on
- 1 tablespoon olive oil
- Sea salt and pepper, to taste
- 1/3 cup brown sugar
- 3 tablespoons fish sauce
- 1 1/2 tablespoon soy sauce
- 2 tablespoons lime juice
- Sea salt and pepper, to taste
- 1 cup vegetable broth

Nutritional Information

301 Calories
8g Fat
13.1g Carbs
0.6g Fiber
44.4g Protein

Directions

Press the "Sauté" button and heat the olive oil. Stir the salt, pepper, brown sugar, fish sauce, soy sauce, lime and vegetable broth. Bring to a simmer and cook until the sauce get thick. Press the "Cancel" button. Reserve.

Then put 1 cup of water, and a metal trivet in the bottom of the inner pot. Place the fish packets on the trivet.

Secure the lid. Choose the "Steam" mode and cook for 3 minutes at Low pressure. When cooking is complete, use a quick pressure release and carefully remove the lid.

Serve the fish fillets and spoon the sauce over.

SOUPS

French Lentil Soup

Ingredients

- 1 cup red lentils, rinsed and drained
- 2 carrots, diced
- 1 large yellow onion, chopped
- 1 can diced tomatoes
- 2 stalks celery, sliced
- 2 tablespoons olive oil
- 1 teaspoon dried oregano
- 5 cups vegetable broth
- 3 garlic cloves, chopped
- 1 tablespoon fresh thyme
- salt and pepper, to taste

Nutritional Information

291 Calories
10.3g Fat
39g Carbs
7.9g Fiber
12.4g Protein

Directions

Preheat your Instant Pot by pressing the "Sauté" button and heat the olive oil. Cook the onion and carrot for 2-3 minutes. Add in the garlic and continue to cook for another 40 seconds.

Stir in the celery, lentils and diced tomatoes. Season with salt, pepper, thyme and oregano. Cook for 1-2 minutes. Then add the vegetable broth.

Secure the lid. Choose the "Manual" mode and cook for 15 minutes at High pressure. When cooking is complete, use a quick pressure release and carefully remove the lid.

Ladle into soup bowls and serve warm. Enjoy!

Rich and Creamy Mushroom Soup

Ingredients

- 1 lb. portobello mushrooms,
- 2 tablespoons butter
- 3 cloves garlic, minced
- 2 shallots, finely chopped
- 1 teaspoon dried thyme
- 4 cups vegetable broth
- salt and ground pepper, to taste
- 1 cup heavy cream
- 1/3 cup fresh parsley, chopped

Nutritional Information

210 Calories
17.4g Fat
10.6g Carbs
1.8g Fiber
4.4g Protein

Directions

Preheat your Instant Pot by pressing the "Sauté" button and melt the butter. Cook the garlic, shallot and thyme until they are aromatic.

Stir in the sliced mushrooms, salt and pepper. Cook until the mushrooms start to reduce their size.

Pour in the vegetable stock and secure the lid. Choose the "Sealing" mode and High pressure; cook for 10 minutes. Use a quick pressure release for 10 minutes and carefully remove the lid.

When pressure is released, carefully transfer the soup to a blender and blend until smooth consistency.

Transfer the soup into the Instant Pot and stir in the cream. Turn your Instant Pot by pressing the "Sauté" button and leave to simmer for 3-4 minutes or until it gets thick.

Serve warm and sprinkle with the fresh parsley.

Tasty Potato Soup with Cheddar Cheese

(Ready in about 20 minutes | Servings 6)

Ingredients

- 3 cloves garlic, minced
- 4 russet potatoes, peeled and cut into cubes
- 1 1/2 onion, chopped
- 1 teaspoon dried thyme
- 2 carrots, sliced
- 1 1/2 tablespoon butter
- 4 cups vegetable broth
- salt and pepper, to taste
- 1 cup heavy cream
- 1 cup cheddar cheese, shredded

Nutritional Information

301 Calories
9.4g Fat
60.6g Carbs
5g Fiber
8.9g Protein

Directions

Preheat your Instant Pot by pressing the "Sauté" button and melt the butter. Saute the onion for 1-2 minutes. Then add in the garlic and thyme until they are aromatic.

Stir in the potatoes, carrots and vegetable broth. Season with salt and pepper

Secure the lid. Choose the "Sealing" mode and High pressure and cook for 10 minutes. Use a quick pressure release and carefully remove the lid.

When pressure is released, carefully transfer the soup to a blender and blend until smooth consistency.

Transfer the soup into the Instant Pot and stir in the cream. Turn your Instant Pot by pressing the "Sauté" button and leave to simmer for 3-4 minutes or until it gets thick.

Serve warm and sprinkle with the cheddar cheese.

Healthy Chicken Soup with Noodles

(Ready in about 20 minutes | Servings 6)

Ingredients

- 2 chicken breasts, boneless, skinless and cut into small chunks
- 1 large yellow onion, diced
- 2 garlic cloves, minced
- 5 cups chicken stock
- 1 teaspoon dried thyme
- 2 tablespoons butter, melted
- 1 teaspoon salt
- 1 teaspoon pepper
- 1 cup egg noodles
- 2 medium carrots, diced
- 1 celery stalk, sliced
- 1 bay leaf
- 1 teaspoon dried basil
- 1/3 cup fresh lemon juice

Nutritional Information

262 Calories
13.4g Fat
10.5g Carbs
1.2g Fiber
21.9g Protein

Directions

Preheat your Instant Pot by pressing the "Sauté" button and melt the butter. Sear the chicken chunks for 2 minutes per side.

Add in add the garlic, onion, carrots and celery. Saute for 2-3 minutes. Season with the pepper, salt, thyme, bay leaf and basil.

Pour in the chicken stock and secure the lid. Choose the "Manual" mode and High pressure; cook for 10 minutes. When cooking is complete, use a quick pressure release and carefully remove the lid.

Then add the egg noodles to the inner pot.

Secure the lid. Choose the "Soup" mode and cook for 5-6 minutes at High pressure until tender. When cooking is complete, use a quick pressure release and carefully remove the lid.

Serve immediately and drizzle with fresh lemon juice.

Aromatic Tomato Soup

(Ready in about 20 minutes | Servings 4)

Ingredients

- 1 tablespoon olive oil
- 1 ½ onion, sliced
- 1 celery stalk, diced
- 2 carrots, diced
- 3 cups chicken broth
- salt and pepper, to taste
- 2 tablespoons fresh basil, chopped
- 1 tablespoon fresh oregano, chopped
- 2 cans tomatoes, diced
- 1/2 cup heavy cream
- 2 cups croutons
- ½ cup parmesan cheese, shredded

Nutritional Information

225 Calories
13.6g Fat
18.6g Carbs
1.8g Fiber
2.5g Protein

Directions

Preheat your Instant Pot by pressing the "Sauté" button and heat the olive oil. Add in the garlic, onion, carrots and celery. Saute for 2-3 minutes. Season with the pepper, salt, fresh basil and fresh oregano.

Stir in the chicken broth and tomato puree. Secure the lid. Choose the "Manual" mode and High pressure; cook for 5 minutes. When cooking is complete, use a quick pressure release and carefully remove the lid.

Then add the heavy cream and seal the lid again. Let it sit for 8 minutes more.

Serve into bowls and top with croutons or with parmesan cheese.

Simple Minestrone Soup

(Ready in about 10 minutes | Servings 4)

Ingredients

- 1 onion, chopped
- 1 stalk celery, diced
- 1 green bell pepper, sliced
- 2 carrots, diced
- 4 cloves garlic, pressed
- 5 cups vegetable broth
- 1 red bell pepper, sliced
- 1 ½ cup pasta, uncooked
- 1 teaspoon dried basil
- 2 tablespoons olive oil
- ½ teaspoon dried oregano
- 1 bay leaf
- salt and pepper, to taste
- 2 cups chickpeas, canned and rinsed

Nutritional Information

262 Calories
13.3g Fat
32.6g Carbs
7.2g Fiber
5.7g Protein

Directions

Preheat your Instant Pot by pressing the "Sauté" button and heat the olive oil. Saute the onions and garlic until fragrant.

Add in the red bell pepper, green bell pepper, carrots, vegetable broth and celery. Saute for 1-2 minutes. Season with the pepper, salt, dried basil, bay leaf and dried oregano.

Secure the lid. Choose the "Manual" mode and High pressure; cook for 6 minutes. When cooking is complete, use a quick pressure release and carefully remove the lid.

Then add the chickpeas and pasta to the inner pot.

Secure the lid. Choose the "Soup" mode and cook for 5 minutes at High pressure until pasta is tender. Once cooking is complete, use a quick pressure release; carefully remove the lid.

Serve immediately and enjoy!

Perfect Vegetable Beef Soup

(Ready in about 20 minutes | Servings 4)

Ingredients

- 2 tablespoons vegetable oil
- 1 lb. beef chuck roast, boneless and cubed
- salt and pepper, to taste
- 1 teaspoon dried rosemary
- 1 tablespoon dried parsley
- 2 small russet potatoes, peeled and cut into small cubes
- 1 onion, chopped
- 1 teaspoon dried oregano
- 2 celery stalks, chopped
- 3 small carrots, chopped
- 3 cloves garlic, chopped
- 4 cups vegetable broth
- 1 cup tomato puree

Nutritional Information

296 Calories
13.6g Fat
19.6g Carbs
4.4g Fiber
27.4g Protein

Directions

Preheat your Instant Pot by pressing the "Sauté" button and heat the vegetable oil. Saute the beef cubes for 3 minutes, stir frequently.

Add in the onions, garlic, potatoes, carrots, vegetable broth, tomato puree and celery. Season with the pepper, salt, oregano, dried parsley and rosemary.

Secure the lid. Choose the "Manual" mode and High pressure; cook for 15 minutes. When cooking is complete, use a quick pressure release and carefully remove the lid.

Serve hot and enjoy!

The Best Cheesy Broccoli Soup

(Ready in about 10 minutes | Servings 4)

Ingredients

- 3 tablespoons butter
- 1/2 teaspoon paprika
- 3 cloves garlic, pressed
- 4 cups vegetable broth
- 5 cups broccoli florets
- salt and pepper, to taste
- 1/2 teaspoon chili powder
- 1 cup heavy cream
- 1 cup cheddar cheese, shredded

Nutritional Information

201 Calories
20.1g Fat
4.6g Carbs
1.8g Fiber
2.7g Protein

Directions

Preheat your Instant Pot by pressing the "Sauté" button and melt the butter. Saute the onion and garlic until fragrant.

Stir in the broccoli, vegetable broth, salt, pepper, paprika

Secure the lid. Choose the "Manual" mode and cook for 4 minutes at High pressure. Once cooking is complete, use a quick pressure release and carefully remove the lid.

Stir in the heavy cream and cheddar cheese. Let it simmer until it gets thick.

Serve warm and add more cheddar on top.

Nutritious Pork Soup

(Ready in about 10 minutes | Servings 5)

Ingredients

- 1 lb. pork tenderloin, cut into cubes
- 2 medium potatoes, peeled and cut into cubes
- 2 tablespoons butter
- 1 red bell pepper, chopped
- 1 teaspoon onion powder
- 2 scallions, chopped
- 1 teaspoon garlic powder
- salt and pepper, to taste
- 1 cup tomato puree
- 5 cups pork stock
- 2 jalapeno peppers, diced

Nutritional Information

276 Calories
7.8g Fat
20g Carbs
2.6g Fiber
31.4g Protein

Directions

Preheat your Instant Pot by pressing the "Sauté" button and melt the butter. Cook the pork cubes for 2-3 minutes, stir occasionally.

Add in the potatoes, red bell pepper, onion powder, scallions, garlic powder, tomato puree, pork stock, salt and pepper.

Secure the lid. Choose the "Manual" mode and cook for 4 minutes at High pressure. When cooking is complete, use a quick pressure release and carefully remove the lid.

Stir in the heavy cream and cheddar cheese. Let it simmer until it gets thick.

Serve hot and garnish with jalapeno pepper.

Colorful Vegetable Soup

(Ready in about 10 minutes | Servings 5)

Ingredients

- 1 large yellow onion, chopped
- 1 red bell pepper, diced
- 4 garlic cloves, minced
- 1 teaspoon dried oregano
- 2 tablespoons vegetable oil
- 2 cups broccoli florets
- 2 carrots, sliced
- ½ cup frozen corn
- 2 cups cauliflower florets
- 1 teaspoon dried basil
- 1 green bell pepper, diced
- 5 cups vegetable broth
- salt and pepper, to taste
- 1 cup croutons

Nutritional Information

184 Calories
9.4g Fat
15.6g Carbs
2.9g Fiber
4g Protein

Directions

Preheat your Instant Pot by pressing the "Sauté" button and heat the vegetable oil. Saute the garlic and onion until fragrant.

Stir in the vegetable broth, carrots, broccoli, cauliflower, red bell pepper, corn and green bell pepper. Season with salt, pepper, dried basil and oregano.

Secure the lid. Choose the "Manual" mode and cook for 5 minutes at High pressure. When cooking is complete, use a quick pressure release and carefully remove the lid.

Serve and garnish with croutons. Bon appetite!

STOCKS & SAUCES

Traditional Chicken Stock

(Ready in about 1 hour 10 minutes | Servings 12)

Ingredients

- 2 pounds chicken wings
- 2 carrots, halved
- 10 cups cold water
- 1 large onion, quartered
- 1 tablespoon salt
- 2 bay leaves
- 6 cloves garlic
- 1 bunch thyme
- 1 bunch parsley

Nutritional Information

85 Calories
2.7g Fat
2g Carbs
0.5g Fiber
23g Protein

Directions

Combine the chicken wings, carrots, onion, salt, water, bay leaves, garlic, thyme and parsley in the inner pot.

Secure the lid. Choose the "Soup/Broth" mode and cook for 40 minutes at High pressure. When cooking is complete, use a quick pressure release for 30 minutes and carefully remove the lid.

Strain the stock and refrigerate until is completely cool.

Nutritious Beef Bone Broth

(Ready in about 2 hours 35 minutes | Servings 8)

Ingredients

- 3 stalks celery, chopped
- 7 cups water
- 1 tablespoon fresh oregano
- 2 onions, sliced
- 2 ½ pounds beef bones
- 1 tablespoon thyme
- 3 carrots, chopped
- 6 cloves garlic, whole
- 1 1/2 teaspoon whole peppercorn
- 1 tablespoon light soy sauce
- 1 tablespoon fresh parsley
- 1 tablespoon apple cider vinegar
- 1 teaspoon Kosher salt
- 1 teaspoon pepper

Nutritional Information

65 Calories
2.4g Fat
4.6g Carbs
0.9g Fiber
6.7g Protein

Directions

Preheat your oven to 400°F and line a baking tray with a baking sheet.

Arrange the carrots, celery, beef bones, onions and garlic on the baking tray. Bake for 35 minutes or until golden brown.

Transfer the vegetables and beef to the inner pot of your Instant Pot. Stir in the light soy sauce, apple cider vinegar and water. Season with salt, pepper, parsley, whole peppercorn, thyme and oregano.

Secure the lid and choose the "Manual" mode and cook for 120 minutes at High pressure. When cooking is complete, leave the instant pot to release its pressure naturally.

Remove the beef bones and vegetables and strain the broth. When the broth is cool, transfer into jars and store in the refrigerator.

Super Vegetable Stock

(Ready in about 50 minutes | Servings 10)

Ingredients

- 3 celery stalks,
- 2 red onions, sliced
- 6 garlic cloves
- 2 bay leaves
- 1/2 cup fresh rosemary, chopped
- 9 cups water
- 1/3 cup fresh thyme, chopped
- salt and pepper, to taste
- 2 tablespoons olive oil
- 1 ½ cup mushrooms
- 4 carrots, cut into halves

Nutritional Information

56 Calories

3.4g Fat

3.2g Carbs

0.4g Fiber

0.3g Protein

Directions

Preheat your oven to 400°F and grease a baking tray with a cooking spray.

Arrange the carrots, celery, mushrooms, red onions and garlic on the baking tray. Season with salt and pepper. Bake for 15 minutes or until golden brown.

Transfer the vegetables the inner pot of your Instant Pot. Stir in the water and season with salt, pepper, rosemary, thyme and bay leaves.

Secure the lid and choose the "Manual" mode and cook for 30 minutes at High pressure. When cooking is complete, leave the instant pot to release its pressure naturally.

Strain the broth and leave to cool before you store it in the refrigerator.

Nourishing Pork Stock

Ingredients

- 1 large parsnip, cut into large chunks
- 1 tablespoon fresh parsley, chopped
- 4 celery stalks, cut into cubes
- 3 bay leaves
- 1 tablespoon lemon juice
- 2 carrots, cut into large circles
- 6 cups water, divided in half
- 1pound pork bones
- 1 tablespoon fresh thyme, chopped
- 6 garlic cloves, smashed
- 2 yellow onions, quartered
- salt and pepper, to taste

Nutritional Information

91 Calories; 4.1g Fat; 3.3g Carbs; 0.4g Fiber; 9.9g Protein

Directions

Arrange the pork bones, celery stalks, carrots, onions, garlic cloves and parsnip on the baking tray. Season with salt and pepper.

Preheat your oven to 450°F and grease a baking tray with a cooking spray and bake for 20 minutes or until golden brown.

Transfer the vegetables to the inner pot of your Instant Pot. Stir in the water and season with salt, pepper, fresh thyme, parsley lemon juice, and bay leaves.

Secure the lid and choose the "Manual" mode and cook for 30 minutes at High pressure. When cooking is complete, leave the instant pot to release its pressure naturally.

Strain the broth and leave to cool before you store it in the refrigerator.

Traditional Fish Stock

(Ready in about 55 minutes | Servings 7)

Ingredients

- 1 carrot, chopped
- 2 onions, cut into chunks
- 2 tablespoons fresh parsley, chopped
- 3 medium salmon heads, washed and cut into quarters
- 2 celery stalks, chopped
- 4 peppercorns
- 1 tablespoon fresh thyme, chopped
- 2 tablespoons vegetable oil
- 7 cups water

Nutritional Information

63 Calories
3.5g Fat
2.7g Carbs
0.7g Fiber
4.9g Protein

Directions

Place the chopped carrot, onions, fresh parsley, salmon heads, celery stalks, peppercorns, fresh thyme, vegetable oil, water, salt and pepper in the inner pot.

Secure the lid and choose the "Soup/Broth" mode and cook for 35 minutes at High pressure. When cooking is complete, use a natural pressure release for 15 minutes and carefully remove the lid.

Strain the vegetables and fish. Leave to cool and enjoy!

Healthy Roma Tomato Sauce

(Ready in about 55 minutes | Servings 6)

Ingredients

- 3 tablespoons vegetable oil
- 5 cloves garlic, minced
- 3 lbs Roma tomatoes, washed and chopped into quarters
- 1 teaspoon dried basil
- 1 tablespoon dried oregano
- ½ teaspoon red pepper flakes
- 2 small onions, quartered
- salt and pepper, to taste
- 2 small carrots, sliced
- 2 tablespoons fresh parsley, chopped
- ½ cup tomato paste

Nutritional Information

115 Calories
7.5g Fat
12.1g Carbs
0.9g Fiber
2.6g Protein

Directions

Preheat your Instant Pot by pressing the "Sauté" button and heat the vegetable oil. Cook the garlic for 30 seconds or until fragrant.

Add in the basil, and oregano, tomatoes, carrots and onions. Season with salt, pepper and red pepper flakes. Stir well.

Secure the lid. Choose the "Manual" mode and cook for 25 minutes at High pressure. When cooking is complete, use a natural pressure release and carefully remove the lid.

Leave the tomato sauce to cool. Then use a food processor to blend the tomato sauce until smooth consistency.

Sprinkle fresh parsley to your tomato sauce and enjoy!

Perfect Peach Sauce

(Ready in about 15 minutes | Servings 8)

Ingredients

- 2 tablespoons fresh lemon juice
- 11/2 teaspoon ground cinnamon
- 1/2 cup brown sugar
- 2 pounds peaches, ripped and chopped
- 1/2 teaspoon ground cardamom
- 1 tablespoon vanilla extract

Nutritional Information

73 Calories
0.1g Fat
19.2g Carbs
0.9g Fiber
0.3g Protein

Directions

Add the peaches, lemon juice, brown sugar, ground cinnamon, ground cardamom and vanilla. Stir well.

Secure the lid. Choose the "Manual" mode and cook for 10 minutes at High pressure. When cooking is complete, use a natural pressure release and carefully remove the lid.

Then for a smoother consistency, you can use a blender.

Serve at room temperature or cold. Enjoy!

Hot Salsa Sauce

(Ready in about 35 minutes | Servings 8)

Ingredients

- 3 small red onions, chopped
- 1 teaspoon dried cumin
- 1 teaspoon pepper
- 5 garlic cloves, pressed
- 2 red bell peppers, sliced
- ½ cup jalapeno peppers, chopped
- 10 cups fresh tomatoes, peeled and diced
- 1/2 cup vinegar
- 1 teaspoon salt
- 2 tablespoons brown sugar
- 2 tablespoons fresh cilantro, chopped

Nutritional Information

83 Calories
0.4g Fat
18.8g Carbs
1.5g Fiber
3.2g Protein

Directions

Place the red onions, garlic cloves, red bell peppers, jalapeno peppers, fresh tomatoes, vinegar, brown sugar, salt, pepper, dried cumin and fresh cilantro into the inner pot of your Instant Pot.

Secure the lid. Choose the "Manual" mode and cook for 30 minutes at High pressure. When cooking is complete, use a natural pressure release and carefully remove the lid.

Leave to cool and store in the refrigerator.

Homemade BBQ Sauce

Ingredients

- 3 tablespoons sesame oil
- 3 onions, chopped
- ½ teaspoon pepper
- 4 cloves garlic, minced
- 1 cup tomato puree
- 2 cups tomato sauce
- 1/2 cup white vinegar
- 1 teaspoon dried cumin
- 3 tablespoons Worcestershire sauce
- 1/3 cup brown sugar
- 1 tablespoon fresh rosemary, chopped
- 1/2 teaspoon paprika
- 1 teaspoon salt
- 1 cup vegetable broth

Directions

Press the "Sauté" button and heat the sesame oil. Sauté the garlic for 30 seconds and stir in the remaining Ingredients. Mix well.

Secure the lid. Choose the "Manual" mode and cook for 10 minutes at High pressure. When cooking is complete, use a natural pressure release and carefully remove the lid.

Let it cool and serve.

Nutritional Information

89 Calories
0.2g Fat
21.9g Carbs
1.1g Fiber
0.2g Protein

Sweet Homemade Cranberry Sauce

(Ready in about 10 minutes | Servings 8)

Ingredients

- 2 pound fresh cranberries, rinsed
- 1/2 cup brown sugar
- 2 tablespoons orange zest
- 1 cup orange juice
- ½ cup maple syrup
- 1 teaspoon cinnamon
- 1 teaspoon vanilla extract
- ½ teaspoon salt

Nutritional Information

134 Calories
0.2g Fat
34g Carbs
1.1g Fiber
0.5g Protein

Directions

Place the cranberries, orange zest, brown sugar, orange juice, maple syrup, cinnamon, vanilla and salt to the inner pot of your Instant Pot. Mix well.

Secure the lid. Choose the "Manual" mode and cook for 4 minutes at High pressure. When cooking is complete, use a natural pressure release and carefully remove the lid.

Serve with your favorite dish and enjoy!

VEGETABLES

Summer Broccoli Salad with Cashew

Ingredients

- 2 carrots, grated
- ½ cup mayonnaise
- 5 cups fresh broccoli florets
- 1 tablespoon fresh lemon juice
- ½ cup yogurt
- ½ cup cashew, chopped
- 1/3 cup dried cranberries
- 1 tablespoon balsamic vinegar
- Salt and pepper, to taste

Nutritional Information

447 Calories
35.8g Fat
26.4g Carbs
1.9g Fiber
10.3g Protein

Directions

Add the steamer basket and 1 cup of water in the inner pot. Place the broccoli florets into the steamer basket.

Secure the lid. Choose the "Manual" mode and cook for 1 minute at High pressure. When cooking is complete, use a quick pressure release and carefully remove the lid.

Leave the broccoli to cool and transfer into a large salad bowl. Stir in the cashew, carrots, dried cranberries, balsamic vinegar, fresh lemon juice, yogurt and mayo.

Mix well and season with salt and pepper. Serve!

Warm Veggie Soup

(Ready in about 30 minutes | Servings 5)

Ingredients

- 1 large yellow onion, diced
- 1 green bell pepper, chopped
- 5 cups vegetable broth
- 2 carrots, peeled and chopped
- 2 large potatoes, cut into cubes
- 1 cup fresh green beans, cut in halves
- 2 celery ribs, chopped
- 1 red bell pepper, chopped
- 1 cup frozen corn
- ½ teaspoons dried thyme
- 1 tablespoon olive oil
- ½ teaspoons dried oregano
- 3 garlic cloves, sliced
- ½ teaspoons dried basil
- 1 can diced tomatoes
- Salt and pepper, to taste

Nutritional Information

178 Calories
3.8g Fat
28.5g Carbs
1.5g Fiber
4.3g Protein

Directions

Preheat your Instant Pot by pressing the "Sauté" button and heat the olive oil. Cook the onion and garlic until fragrant.

With a wooden spoon remove any left brown bits. Add the potatoes, red bell pepper, carrots, celery, green bell pepper, corn and diced tomatoes. Season with salt, pepper, thyme, basil and oregano.

Secure the lid. Choose the "Manual" mode and cook for 14 minutes at High pressure. When cooking is complete, use a natural pressure release for 10 minutes and carefully remove the lid.

Stir in the green beans and press the "Sauté" button again. Cook on the lowest setting for 5-6 minutes. Serve!

Mom's Veggie Sweet Potato Chili

(Ready in about 10 minutes | Servings 4)

Ingredients

- 2 tablespoons butter
- 2 cloves garlic, minced
- 2 carrots, cut into 1-inch pieces
- 1/3 cup fresh parsley, chopped
- 1 can black beans, rinsed and drained
- 2 tablespoons fresh cilantro, chopped
- 1 large yellow onion, chopped
- 3 sweet potatoes, peeled and cut into cubes
- 1 teaspoon chili powder
- 2 cups vegetable broth
- 1 teaspoon cumin
- 1 can tomato sauce
- salt and pepper, to taste

Nutritional Information

114 Calories
8g Fat
10.7g Carbs
2.7g Fiber
1.4g Protein

Directions

Preheat your Instant Pot by pressing the "Sauté" button and melt the butter. Cook the onion and garlic until fragrant.

Stir in the carrots, fresh cilantro, sweet potatoes, chili powder, vegetable broth, cumin, tomato sauce, salt and pepper.

Secure the lid. Choose the "Manual" mode and cook for 8 minutes at High pressure. When cooking is complete, use a quick pressure release and carefully remove the lid.

Stir in the black beans and press the "Sauté" button again. Cook on the lowest setting for 10 minutes. Serve hot!

Roasted Brussels Sprouts with Honey

(Ready in about 10 minutes | Servings 2)

Ingredients

- 1 pound Brussels sprouts, washed, trimmed and cut into halves
- 1 tablespoon olive oil
- 1 teaspoon garlic, minced
- 1 large yellow onion, chopped
- Salt and pepper, to taste
- 1/2 teaspoon red pepper flakes
- 2 tablespoons honey

Nutritional Information

290 Calories
12.2g Fat
43.7g Carbs
9.9g Fiber
8.7g Protein

Directions

Add the steamer basket and 1 cup of water to the inner pot. Place the Brussels sprouts in the steamer basket.

Secure the lid. Choose the "Steam" mode and cook for 3 minutes at High pressure. When cooking is complete, use a quick pressure release and carefully remove the lid. Then drain the water out of the inner pot.

Press the "Sauté" button and heat the olive oil. Saute the garlic and onion until aromatic and add the Brussels sprouts, salt, pepper and red pepper flakes. Stir well.

Drizzle with honey and serve warm!

Fluffy Potato Salad

(Ready in about 15 minutes + chilling time | Servings 5)

Ingredients

- 1 cup mayonnaise
- 1/3 cup scallions, chopped
- 2 pounds small Russet potatoes, peeled and cubed
- 1 1/2 tablespoon mustard
- 4 boiled eggs, peeled and chopped
- 1 ½ tablespoon fresh parsley, chopped
- Salt and pepper, to taste
- ½ teaspoon red pepper

Nutritional Information

379 Calories
21.7g Fat
36.3g Carbs
3.5g Fiber
12.2g Protein

Directions

Add 1 cup of water and a metal trivet to the inner pot of your Instant Pot. Place the potatoes in a steamer basket and lower the steamer basket onto the trivet.

Secure the lid. Choose the "Manual" mode and cook for 8 minutes at High pressure. When cooking is complete, use a quick pressure release and carefully remove the lid.

Remove the steamer basket and leave the potatoes to cool.

In a large bowl add the potatoes, scallions, mayonnaise, mustard, eggs, parsley, red pepper, salt and pepper. Stir well.

Serve and enjoy!

Moroccan-Style Eggplant with Lentils

Ingredients

- 1 yellow onion, chopped
- 1 cup lentils, boiled and rinsed
- 1 red bell pepper, deseeded and diced
- 1 lb. eggplant, cut into cubes
- 1 green bell pepper, deseeded and diced
- 3 garlic cloves, sliced
- 1/2 teaspoon oregano
- 1/2 teaspoon basil
- 1 teaspoon paprika
- Salt and pepper, to taste
- 2 tablespoons sesame oil

Nutritional Information

258 Calories
13g Fat
30.5g Carbs
11.4g Fiber
8.3g Protein

Directions

Sprinkle the eggplant cubes with salt and place them in a colander. Let it sit for 25 minutes. Then rinse with water and dry.

Press the "Sauté" button and heat the sesame oil. Saute the onion until translucent. Then add the garlic, eggplant cubes, green and red bell peppers and garlic. Cook for 2-3 minutes.

Stir in the lentils, tomatoes, oregano, basil, paprika, salt and pepper. Mix well.

Secure the lid. Choose the "Manual" mode and cook for 3 minutes at High pressure. When cooking is complete, use a quick pressure release and carefully remove the lid.

Serve into bowls. Bon appetite!

Sweet Baby Carrots

Ingredients

- 4 tablespoons butter
- 1/2 teaspoon salt
- 3 lbs. baby carrots
- 3 tablespoons honey
- 1/3 teaspoon cinnamon
- ½ teaspoon dried thyme
- 1/3 teaspoon pepper
- 1 ½ cup water

Nutritional Information

135 Calories
6.8g Fat
20.7g Carbs
5.2g Fiber
1.4g Protein

Directions

Place a steamer basket and 1 cup of water to the inner pot of your Instant Pot. Add the carrots in the steamer basket.

Secure the lid. Choose the "Steam" mode and cook for 3 minutes at High pressure. When cooking is complete, use a quick pressure release and carefully remove the lid.

Remove the water and press the "Sauté" button. Stir in the butter, cinnamon, thyme and honey. Saute for 1 minute then add in the cooked carrots, pepper, and salt.

Cook for 2-3 minutes and serve warm. Bon appetite!

Steamed Green Beans with Mayo

Ingredients

- 1 lb. green beans, trimmed and cut in half
- 1/2 cup mayonnaise
- 2 garlic cloves, pressed
- 1 tablespoon yogurt
- 2 tablespoons fresh parsley, minced
- 1 tablespoon green onion, finely chopped
- Salt and pepper, to taste
- 1 cup water

Nutritional Information

187 Calories
13.4g Fat
12.7g Carbs
6.4g Protein
4.5g Sugars

Directions

Place a steamer basket and 1 cup of water to the inner pot of your Instant Pot. Add the green beans in the steamer basket.

Season them with salt and pepper. Then lower the steamer basket into the inner pot.

Secure the lid. Choose the "Manual" mode and cook for 2 minutes at High pressure. When cooking is complete, use a quick pressure release and carefully remove the lid.

Meanwhile, mix the mayonnaise with the onion, garlic, yogurt and parsley. Serve the green beans with the mayo dip on the side. Bon appétit!

Sunday Vegetable Mix

(Ready in about 10 minutes | Servings 5)

Ingredients

- 2 tablespoons butter
- 4 cloves garlic, minced
- 2 carrots, cut into circles
- ½ lb. green beans
- 1 large yellow onion, sliced
- ½ lb. broccoli florets
- 2 medium sweet potatoes, peeled and cubed
- ½ cup corn
- 2 cups vegetable broth
- 2 tablespoons fresh parsley, chopped

Nutritional Information

182 Calories
5.9g Fat
29.8g Carbs
5.5g Protein
4.5g Sugars

Directions

Press the "Sauté" button and melt the butter. Then sauté the garlic until fragrant.

Stir in the carrots, onion, green beans, corn, broccoli florets, sweet potatoes and vegetable broth.

Secure the lid. Choose the "Manual" mode and cook for 5 minutes at High pressure. When cooking is complete, use a quick pressure release and carefully remove the lid.

Sprinkle with fresh parsley and serve warm. Bon appétit!

SIDE DISHES

Super Easy Corn on the Cob

Ingredients

- 4 tablespoons butter
- 3 ears corn on the cob, husked and silk removed
- 1/3 cup parmesan cheese, grated
- salt and pepper, to taste

Nutritional Information

311 Calories
19.4g Fat
32.5g Carbs
3.8g Fiber
7.7g Protein

Directions

Place the metal trivet to the inner pot and pour in 1 cup of water.

Place your corn on the trivet.

Secure the lid. Choose the "Manual" mode and cook for 3 minutes at High pressure. When cooking is complete, use a quick pressure release and carefully remove the lid.

Slather with butter and sprinkle with parmesan cheese and salt.

Enjoy!

Sweet Potatoes with Cheddar Cheese

(Ready in about 30 minutes | Servings 4)

Ingredients

- 4 sweet potatoes, washed and scrubbed
- 1 cup water
- ½ cup cheddar cheese, shredded
- 1/3 cup scallion, finely sliced
- 3 tablespoons butter

Nutritional Information

184 Calories
8.8g Fat
24.2g Carbs
4g Fiber
2.5g Protein

Directions

Place a metal trivet in the inner pot of your Instant Pot and pour 1 cup of water. Place the potatoes on the trivet.

Secure the lid. Choose the "Steam" mode and cook for 15 minutes at High pressure. When cooking is complete, use a natural pressure release for 15 minutes and carefully remove the lid.

Slice the sweet potatoes into halves and top with butter, scallions and cheddar cheese.

Serve immediately. Bon appetite!

Lazy Eggplant with Mayo-Lemon Dressing

(Ready in about 10 minutes | Servings 4)

Ingredients

- 3 medium eggplants, sliced into rings
- 2 tablespoons olive oil
- salt, to taste
- 1 cup water
- 4 tablespoons mayonnaise
- ½ teaspoon garlic powder
- ½ teaspoon fresh lemon juice
- fresh basil, for serving

Nutritional Information

212 Calories
12.6g Fat
24.9g Carbs
12.5g Fiber
5g Protein

Directions

Salt the eggplant rings on both sides.

Press the "Sauté" button and heat the olive oil. Saute the eggplant until light brown and add 1 cup of water to the inner pot.

Secure the lid. Choose the "Manual" mode and cook for 3 minutes at High pressure. When cooking is complete, use a quick pressure release and carefully remove the lid.

In a small bowl mix the mayonnaise, lemon juice, salt and garlic powder. Stir well.

Serve the eggplant rings and top with the dressing.

Steamed Broccoli with Garlic and Lemon

Ingredients

- 1 ½ lb. broccoli florets
- 5 garlic cloves, diced
- 1 cup water
- salt and pepper, to taste
- 1 tablespoon sesame seed
- 4 lemon slices
- salt and pepper, to taste

Nutritional Information

101 Calories
3g Fat
15.8g Carbs
7.3g Fiber
8.7g Protein

Directions

Place the steamer basket to the inner pot and add 1 cup of water. Stir in the broccoli florets in the steamer basket.

Secure the lid. Choose the "Manual" mode and cook for 1 minute at High pressure. When cooking is complete, use a quick pressure release and carefully remove the lid.

Serve the broccoli and sprinkle with the diced garlic, salt, pepper and lemon slices.

Enjoy!

Fast Black-Eyed Peas with Ham

(Ready in about 35 minutes | Servings 4)

Ingredients

- 1 ½ cups dry black-eyed peas
- ½ cup ham, diced
- 1 large onion, diced
- 3 cups vegetable stock
- 1/3 teaspoon dried oregano
- 1/4 teaspoon dried sage
- salt and pepper, to taste
- 1 red bell pepper, diced
- 1 ½ tablespoon olive oil

Nutritional Information

148 Calories
10.6g Fat
8.5g Carbs
1.1g Fiber
5.1g Protein

Directions

Preheat your Instant Pot by pressing the "Sauté" button and heat the olive oil. Saute the onion and red bell pepper until translucent.

Season with salt, pepper, dried sage and oregano. Mix well.

Stir in the ham, black-eyed peas and vegetable broth.

Secure the lid. Choose the "Manual" mode and cook for 17 minutes at High pressure. When cooking is complete, use a natural pressure release for 15 minutes and carefully remove the lid.

Serve into bowls and enjoy!

Favorite Fried Cabbage with Bacon

(Ready in about 10 minutes | Servings 4)

Ingredients

- 1 head of cabbage, cored and roughly chopped
- 1/2 cup green onions, sliced
- salt and pepper, to taste
- 1 tablespoon olive oil
- 2 cloves garlic, minced
- 1 ½ cup vegetable broth
- 1 bay leaf
- 4 slices bacon, cut into cubes
- ½ teaspoon paprika

Nutritional Information

194 Calories
13.9g Fat
14g Carbs
3.5g Fiber
5.6g Protein

Directions

Preheat your Instant Pot by pressing the "Sauté" button and heat the olive oil. Saute the bacon until done and set aside.

Remove any brown bits from the instant pot with a wooden spoon.

Add to the instant pot the chopped cabbage, vegetable broth, green onion, salt, pepper, garlic, bay leaf and paprika. Stir well.

Season with salt, pepper, dried sage and oregano. Mix well.

Secure the lid. Choose the "Manual" mode and cook for 3 minutes at High pressure. When cooking is complete, use a quick pressure release.

Serve the cabbage and sprinkle with the bacon cubes.

Wild Mushroom Rice

(Ready in about 35 minutes | Servings 4)

Ingredients

- 2 tablespoons olive oil
- 1 large onion, finely chopped
- 4 cloves garlic, sliced
- 2 cups basmati rice
- 2 cups vegetable stock
- salt and pepper, to taste
- 1 bay leaf
- 1 ½ cup mushrooms, chopped
- ½ teaspoon thyme
- 1 teaspoon red pepper flakes

Nutritional Information

284 Calories
19.2g Fat
37.6g Carbs
13.8g Fiber
9.7g Protein

Directions

Preheat your Instant Pot by pressing the "Sauté" button and heat the olive oil. Saute the onion, mushrooms and garlic until fragrant.

Add the basmati rice, vegetable broth, bay leaf, thyme, red pepper flakes, salt and pepper to the inner pot.

Secure the lid. Choose the "Manual" mode and cook for 20 minutes at High pressure. When cooking is complete, use a natural pressure release for 10 minutes and carefully remove the lid.

Serve warm in individual bowls.

Simple Pepper Fajitas

(Ready in about 10 minutes | Servings 3)

Ingredients

- 2 green bell peppers, seeded and sliced into strips
- salt and pepper, to taste
- 2 large onions, diced
- 1/2 cup vegetable broth
- 2 orange bell peppers, seeded and sliced into strips
- 1 cup tomato sauce
- 2 tablespoons vegetable oil
- 1 teaspoon paprika
- ½ cup fresh parsley, finely diced

Nutritional Information

253 Calories
9.7g Fat
36.6g Carbs
8.9g Fiber
5.2g Protein

Directions

Preheat your Instant Pot by pressing the "Sauté" button and heat the vegetable oil. Saute the peppers and onions until tender.

Stir in the vegetable broth, tomato sauce, salt, pepper and paprika.

Secure the lid. Choose the "Manual" mode and cook for 3 minutes at High pressure. When cooking is complete, use a quick pressure release and carefully remove the lid.

Sprinkle fresh parsley over your peppers and serve.

Nutritious Green Beans with Ham

Ingredients

- 5 cups green beans, cut into halves
- 1 large onion, diced
- 2 tablespoons olive oil
- 4 garlic cloves, minced
- 1 cup ham, diced
- 1/2 cup water
- 1 ½ tablespoon soy sauce
- 1 tablespoon sesame seeds
- Salt pepper, to taste

Nutritional Information

179 Calories
10.8g Fat
15.8g Carbs
4.9g Fiber
7.6g Protein

Directions

Preheat your Instant Pot by pressing the "Sauté" button and heat the olive oil. Saute the ham, garlic and onions until fragrant.

Stir the green beans, soy sauce salt, pepper and water the inner pot.

Secure the lid. Choose the "Manual" mode and cook for 3 minutes at High pressure. When cooking is complete, use a quick pressure release and carefully remove the lid.

Sprinkle with the sesame seeds and serve.

Special Mashed Potatoes

Ingredients

- 3 pounds potatoes, peeled and diced
- 1 cup water
- 1 teaspoon salt
- 1 large red onion, chopped
- 2 tablespoons fresh parsley leaves, roughly chopped
- 1/3 cup sour cream
- 2 tablespoons butter

Nutritional Information

226 Calories
5.4g Fat
40.6g Carbs
5g Fiber
5.1g Protein

Directions

Add the water and potatoes to the Instant Pot.

Secure the lid. Choose the "Manual" mode and cook for 10 minutes at High pressure. When cooking is complete, use a quick pressure release and carefully remove the lid.

Drain the water from the potatoes. Using a potato masher, mash the potatoes.

Add the butter, salt, red onion and sour cream. Then sprinkle with fresh parsley and serve.

EGGS & DAIRY

Steamed Cauliflower with Cheese Dip

(Ready in about 10 minutes | Servings 3)

Ingredients

- 1/2 cup mayonnaise
- 1 teaspoon garlic, pressed
- 1 tablespoon sour cream
- 1 lb. cauliflower, broken into florets
- ½ cup blue cheese
- 1 cup water
- Salt and pepper, to taste

Nutritional Information

259 Calories
20.8g Fat
11.6g Carbs
3.8g Fiber
10.2g Protein

Directions

Add the steamer basket and 1 cup of water to the inner pot. Place the cauliflower in the steamer basket.

Secure the lid. Choose the "Steam" mode and cook for 2 minutes at High pressure. When cooking is complete, use a quick pressure release and carefully remove the lid.

In a bowl mix the mayonnaise, garlic, blue cheese, sour cream, salt and pepper. Stir until smooth consistency is reached.

Serve the cauliflower with the cheese dip on the side.

Mini Frittatas with Cheddar

(Ready in about 10 minutes | Servings 3)

Ingredients

- 6 eggs
- 1/3 cup coconut milk
- 2 green onions, chopped
- salt and pepper, to taste
- 1/2 cup cheddar cheese

Nutritional Information

294 Calories
20.4g Fat
7.6g Carbs
1.1g Fiber
19.6g Protein

Directions

In a large bowl combine the eggs, coconut milk, green onions, cheddar cheese, salt and pepper. Mix well.

Pour the egg mixture into silicone molds. Then place 1 cup of water and a metal trivet in the inner pot. Lower the molds onto the prepared trivet.

Secure the lid. Choose the "Manual" mode and cook for 5 minutes at High pressure. When cooking is complete, use a quick pressure release and carefully remove the lid.

Serve warm. Bon appetite!

Classic Stuffed Eggs

Ingredients

- 1/4 cup mayonnaise
- 1 teaspoon red pepper
- 2 tablespoons fresh chives, minced
- 1 tablespoon Dijon mustard
- 8 eggs
- salt and pepper, to taste

Nutritional Information

315 Calories
24.3g Fat
3.9g Carbs
0.5g Fiber
19.2g Protein

Directions

Place 1 cup of water and a steamer rack in the inner pot and arrange the eggs on the rack.

Secure the lid. Choose the "Manual" mode and cook for 5 minutes at High pressure. When cooking is complete, use a quick pressure release and carefully remove the lid.

Peel and slice the eggs into halves. Remove the yolks.

In a large bowl combine the egg yolks, mayonnaise, fresh chives, Dijon mustard, salt and pepper. Mix well. Fill each of the egg halves with the mixture.

Serve and sprinkle with red pepper. Bon appetite!

Japanese Fluffy Pancake

(Ready in about 25 minutes | Servings 4)

Ingredients

- 1 ½ teaspoons baking powder
- 2 tablespoons brown sugar
- 1 ½ cup all-purpose flour
- 1 teaspoon salt
- 1 ½ cup milk
- 2 eggs, whisked
- 1/3 cup maple syrup
- ½ cup fresh berries

Nutritional Information

439 Calories
9.8g Fat
74.6g Carbs
1.8g Fiber
12.9g Protein

Directions

Add 1 cup of water and a metal trivet to the inner pot. Then line the bottom of a form pan with parchment paper. Grease the bottom and sides of the pan with cooking spray.

In a large bowl mix the flour, salt, milk, eggs, brown sugar and baking powder.

Pour the mixture into the prepared pan and lower the pan onto the trivet.

Secure the lid. Choose the "Manual" mode and cook for 40 minutes at High pressure. When cooking is complete, use a natural pressure release and carefully remove the lid.

Leave to rest and top with the maple syrup and fresh berries. Enjoy!

Cheesy Frittata with Ham

(Ready in about 15 minutes | Servings 4)

Ingredients

- 1 cup ham, sliced into cubes
- 1/3 cup heavy cream
- 1/2 cup cheddar cheese, grated
- ½ cup parmesan cheese
- 1/2 cup feta cheese, cut into small cubes
- salt and pepper, to taste
- 2 tablespoons olive oil
- 7 eggs
- 1 yellow onion, finely chopped

Nutritional Information

446 Calories
37.4g Fat
7.7g Carbs
0.6g Fiber
23.8g Protein

Directions

In a large bowl mix the eggs, ham, heavy cream, cheddar cheese, salt, pepper, parmesan cheese, yellow onion, and feta cheese. Stir well.

Grease a baking dish with the olive oil. Pour the mixture in the baking dish.

Place 1 cup of water and a metal trivet in the inner pot. Lower the baking dish onto the prepared trivet.

Secure the lid. Choose the "Manual" mode and cook for 6 minutes at High pressure. When cooking is complete, use a quick pressure release and carefully remove the lid.

Leave to cool and cut carefully. Serve!

Monday Mac and Cheese

(Ready in about 15 minutes | Servings 8)

Ingredients

- 1 ½ pound shells macaroni
- 1 cup fontina cheese, shredded
- 3 tablespoons butter
- 2 cups cheddar cheese, shredded
- salt, to taste
- 3 cups water
- 1 cup milk
- 1/2 cup Parmesan cheese, shredded

Nutritional Information

526 Calories
23.4g Fat
66.6g Carbs
2.7g Fiber
24.8g Protein

Directions

Place the butter, shells macaroni, salt, and water into the inner pot.

Secure the lid. Choose the "Manual" mode and cook for 5 minutes at High pressure. When cooking is complete, use a quick pressure release and carefully remove the lid.

Then add in the milk, cheddar cheese, parmesan and fontina cheese. Stir until it gets thick.

Serve and Bon appetite!

Perfect Hard-Boiled Eggs

Ingredients

- 1/2 teaspoon salt
- 8 medium eggs
- 1 teaspoon red pepper
- ½ teaspoon pepper
- 1 tablespoon fresh dill, finely chopped

Nutritional Information

133 Calories
8.4g Fat
2.6g Carbs
0.5g Fiber
11.4g Protein

Directions

Place a steamer rack in the inner pot and pour 1 cup of water. Arrange the eggs on the rack.

Secure the lid. Choose the "Manual" mode and cook for 5 minutes at High pressure. When cooking is complete, use a quick pressure release and carefully remove the lid.

Place the eggs into cold water and leave to cool for 10 minutes.

Peel your eggs and cut them into halves. Season with salt, pepper, red pepper.

Serve and sprinkle with fresh dill.

Homemade Vanilla Yogurt

(Ready in about 9 hours | Servings 6)

Ingredients

- 1/3 teaspoon salt
- 2 tablespoons prepared yogurt with cultures
- 6 cups whole milk
- 1 ½ tablespoon vanilla

Nutritional Information

232 Calories
7.4g Fat
32.4g Carbs
0.1g Fiber
7.8g Protein

Directions

Add the whole milk into the inner pot. Press the "Yogurt" button and adjust the temperature until the screen reads "Boil".

Carefully remove the lid and leave the milk to reach 100 degrees F. Whisk in the prepared yogurt with the cultures and add the salt and vanilla. Add the inner pot back to the Instant Pot.

Secure the lid. Choose the "Yogurt" mode and set it for 8 hours. When the cycle is complete, remove the lid.

Transfer the prepared yogurt into glass jars and refrigerate.

Instant Spinach Dip

Ingredients

- 1 ½ package frozen spinach
- 1 cup double cream
- 1 teaspoon garlic powder
- 1/3 cup vegetable broth
- salt, to taste
- ½ teaspoon onion powder
- 1 cup Parmesan cheese, shredded
- 1 cup Monterey Jack cheese, grated

Nutritional Information

152 Calories
11.6g Fat
4.5g Carbs
1.3g Fiber
8.3g Protein

Directions

Place the frozen spinach, double cream, garlic powder, onion powder, vegetable broth and salt in the inner pot of your Instant Pot. Stir well.

Secure the lid. Choose the "Manual" mode and cook for 3 minutes at Low pressure. When cooking is complete, use a natural pressure release for 10 minutes and carefully remove the lid.

Add in the parmesan cheese and Monterey Jack cheese. Mix well.

Serve immediately. Bon appetite!

Grandma's Cheese Dip

(Ready in about 5 minutes | Servings 10)

Ingredients

- 1 teaspoon chili powder
- salt and pepper, to taste
- 2 1/2 tablespoons tapioca starch
- 1/3 cup butter
- 2 1/2 cups Cheddar cheese, grated
- 2 cups whole milk

Nutritional Information

224 Calories
17.1g Fat
9.3g Carbs
0.2g Fiber
8.4g Protein

Directions

Press the "Sauté" button and melt the butter. Add in the tapioca starch and the milk. Mix well.

Stir in the salt, pepper and chili powder. Bring to a boil for 2-3 minutes and press the "Cancel" button. Then add in the cheddar cheese and stir until well combined.

Serve warm and enjoy!

Mexican Style Dip

Ingredients

- 1 teaspoon garlic powder
- 3 tablespoons all-purpose flour
- 1 ½ cup whole milk
- 3 tablespoons butter
- 2 cups Monterey Jack, shredded
- Kosher salt, to taste
- 1 ½ cup cheddar cheese, shredded
- 1 teaspoon onion powder
- 1 teaspoon chili pepper
- ½ teaspoon cumin
- ½ teaspoon red pepper flakes
- tortilla chips for serving, optional

Nutritional Information

245 Calories
18.3g Fat
8g Carbs
0.3g Fiber
12.1g Protein

Directions

Press the "Sauté" button and melt the butter. Add the flour, garlic powder, cumin, salt, onion powder, chili pepper and red pepper flakes. Stir well.

Gradually pour in the milk, stirring continuously. Bring to a boil for 3-4 minutes and press the "Cancel" button.

Add in the Monterey Jack cheese and cheddar cheese. Stir until the cheese has melted.

Serve warm with chips (optional). Bon appetite!

DESSERTS

Chocolate Banana Bread

Ingredients

- 3 small eggs
- 1 teaspoon vanilla extract
- 1 cup brown sugar
- 1 ½ teaspoon baking soda
- 2 ½ bananas, mashed
- 1/3 cup butter
- 1 ½ cups flour
- ½ cup almonds, chopped
- 1 cup chocolate chips

Nutritional Information

334 Calories
9.8g Fat
64.6g Carbs
2.7g Fiber
5.6g Protein

Directions

In a large bowl add the sugar, eggs, butter and vanilla. Mix with a hand mixer. Then stir in the mashed bananas and combine well.

In another bowl mix the flour and baking soda. Add gradually the dry mixture to the egg mixture and stir well with a mixer.

When the mixture is combined well, add the chopped almonds and chocolate chips.

Add 1 cup of water and a metal trivet to the bottom of the inner pot. Spritz a baking pan with nonstick cooking oil.

Pour the batter into the prepared pan and place the pan lower onto the trivet.

Secure the lid. Choose the "Manual" mode and cook for 50 minutes at High pressure. When cooking is complete, use a quick pressure release and carefully remove the lid.

Leave the banana bread to cool and serve. Bon appetite!

Light Crème Brulee

(Ready in about 30 minutes | Servings 4)

Ingredients

- 7 egg yolks
- 1 ½ cup heavy cream
- 1/2 cup sugar
- 2 tablespoons whole milk
- 2 teaspoons vanilla
- 1/3 teaspoon salt
- 2 teaspoons brown sugar, for caramelizing

Nutritional Information

311 Calories
24.5g Fat
16.3.6g Carbs
0g Fiber
5.6g Protein

Directions

Place a metal trivet into your Instant Pot and add 1 cup of water.

Heat a large saucepan and stir in the cream and milk. Simmer for 2-3 minutes and leave to cool.

In a medium bowl combine the egg yolks, sugar, vanilla and salt. Then stir in the prepared mixture into the hot cream mixture. Pour the mixture into ramekins. Place the ramekins onto the trivet.

Secure the lid. Choose the "Manual" mode and cook for 11 minutes at High pressure. When cooking is complete, use a natural pressure release for 10 minutes and carefully remove the lid.

Leave to cool overnight. Sprinkle the cream with ½ teaspoon brown sugar and caramelize the sugar, using a kitchen torch. Serve and enjoy!

Afternoon Chocolate Pudding

(Ready in about 20 minutes | Servings 5)

Ingredients

- 2 cups whipping cream
- 1/2 cup brown sugar
- 1 teaspoon vanilla
- ½ teaspoon salt
- 5 egg yolks
- ½ cup water
- 1 ½ tablespoon cacao
- 1 cup dark chocolate, chopped

Nutritional Information

325 Calories
10.5g Fat
52.7g Carbs
1.6g Fiber
4.7g Protein

Directions

Place a metal trivet into your Instant Pot and add ½ cup of water.

Heat a large saucepan and stir in the cream and vanilla. Simmer for a few minutes and then add the dark chocolate. Stir until the chocolate is melted and leave to rest.

Then in a large bowl combine the egg yolks, sugar, cacao and salt. Slowly add the chocolate mixture into the egg mixture.

Pour the mixture into jars. Place the jars onto the trivet.

Secure the lid. Choose the "Manual" mode and cook for 6 minutes at High pressure. When cooking is complete, use a natural pressure release and carefully remove the lid.

Take out the jars and leave to cool. Serve and enjoy!

Summary Strawberry Compote

(Ready in about 15 minutes | Servings 2)

Ingredients

- 1 ½ pound strawberries, washed and trimmed
- 1/2 cup brown sugar
- 2 tablespoons orange juice
- 1 vanilla bean
- 2 cups water

Nutritional Information

214 Calories
1.5g Fat
53g Carbs
6.9g Fiber
2.4g Protein

Directions

Cut the strawberries into halves and place them into the inner pot. Sprinkle with the sugar and let sit for 10 minutes.

Stir in the orange juice, water and vanilla bean.

Secure the lid. Choose the "Manual" mode and cook for 1 minute at High pressure. When cooking is complete, use a natural pressure release and carefully remove the lid.

Place into jars and leave to cool. Serve!

Thick Rice Pudding Dessert

(Ready in about 20 minutes | Servings 4)

Ingredients

- 1 cup water
- ½ teaspoon salt
- 1 teaspoon cinnamon
- 2 ½ cups whole milk
- 1 ½ cup jasmine rice
- 6 tablespoons brown sugar
- 1 teaspoon vanilla extract
- 4 tablespoons pistachios, crushed

Nutritional Information

372 Calories
17.4g Fat
56.4g Carbs
10.4g Fiber
12.3g Protein

Directions

Add the water, rice, vanilla and salt in the inner pot of your Instant Pot.

Secure the lid. Choose the "Rice" mode and cook for 10 minutes at Low pressure. When cooking is complete, use a natural pressure release and carefully remove the lid.

Stir in the pistachios, milk, brown sugar and cinnamon. Mix well.

Press the "Sauté" button and cook, stirring continuously, until the desired consistency is reached.

Press the "Cancel' button and serve into bowls. Bon appetite!

Soft Baked Apples with Honey

(Ready in about 10 minutes | Servings 5)

Ingredients

- 1/3 cup raisins
- 1 teaspoon ground cinnamon
- 1 teaspoon vanilla
- 5 apples, washed and cored
- 3 tablespoons honey
- 1/3 cup chopped walnuts
- 1 cup water

Nutritional Information

171 Calories
3.7g Fat
36.8g Carbs
5g Fiber
1.4g Protein

Directions

Pour the water in the inner pot of your Instant Pot.

In a small bowl mix the walnuts, honey, vanilla, cinnamon and raisins. Stir well.

With a spoon fill the apples with the mixture. Place the apples on the trivet in your Instant Pot.

Secure the lid. Choose the "Manual" mode and cook for 5 minutes at High pressure. When cooking is complete, use a quick pressure release and carefully remove the lid.

Leave to rest and serve!

Light Pumpkin Pudding

Ingredients

- 1 ½ can pumpkin puree
- 1 teaspoon vanilla
- 1/4 teaspoon ground cardamom
- 1/2 cup brown sugar
- 1/2 teaspoon ground cinnamon
- 3 tablespoons flour
- 3 eggs
- 2 ½ tablespoons butter, melted
- 1 cup water
- whipped cream, for garnish

Nutritional Information

266 Calories
14.7g Fat
25.6g Carbs
3g Fiber
8.4g Protein

Directions

Pour 1 cup of water and metal trivet to the bottom of the inner pot of your Instant Pot.

In a large bowl add the eggs, sugar, vanilla, cardamom, cinnamon, flour, melted butter and pumpkin puree. Use a mixer and mix until smooth consistency.

Spray a baking pan with cooking spray. Pour the pumpkin mixture into the baking dish.

Add 1 cup of water and metal trivet to the bottom of the inner pot; cover with a paper towel

Secure the lid. Choose the "Manual" mode and cook for 17 minutes at High pressure. When cooking is complete, use a natural pressure release and carefully remove the lid.

Serve and top with whipped cream.

Simple Pistachio Cheesecake

(Ready in about 40 minutes | Servings 6)

Ingredients

- 1 ½ cup pretzels, crushed
- 1/2 teaspoon vanilla
- 4 tablespoons butter, melted
- 2 cups cream cheese
- 3 small eggs
- 1/3 cup sour cream
- 1 cup brown sugar
- 1/3 cup pistachio, crushed
- A pinch of salt
- 1 cup water
- 1 cup fresh raspberries

Nutritional Information

588 Calories
37.4g Fat
52.6g Carbs
2.6g Fiber
12.6g Protein

Directions

Spray a baking pan with a nonstick cooking spray.

In a large bowl mix the crushed pretzels, pistachios and butter. Press the crust into the prepared baking pan.

In another bowl combine the cream cheese, brown sugar, eggs, sour cream, vanilla and a pinch of salt. Pour this mixture over the crust and cover it with a piece of foil.

Add 1 cup of water and metal trivet to the bottom of the inner pot and lower the baking pan onto the trivet.

Secure the lid. Choose the "Manual" mode and cook for 25 minutes at High pressure. When cooking is complete, use a natural pressure release and carefully remove the lid.

Top with fresh raspberries and serve. Bon appetite!

Fragrant Peach Butter

Ingredients

- 6 large peaches, pitted, peeled and sliced
- ½ cup granulated sugar
- 1 teaspoon vanilla
- 2 tablespoons lemon juice
- 2 teaspoons cornstarch
- 1/3 cup water

Nutritional Information

97 Calories
0.3g Fat
23.8g Carbs
2.3g Fiber
1.9g Protein

Directions

Place the sliced peaches, water, sugar, and vanilla in the inner pot of your Instant Pot.

Secure the lid. Choose the "Manual" mode and cook for 20 minutes at High pressure. When cooking is complete, use a natural pressure release for 10 minutes and carefully remove the lid.

Stir in the lemon juice and cornstarch. Blend in a food processor.

Then leave to rest and store into airtight containers.

Mini Choco Muffins

(Ready in about 25 minutes | Servings 6)

Ingredients

- 1/3 cup butter, melted
- 1/3 cup brown sugar
- 2 large eggs
- 3 tablespoons milk
- 1 teaspoon vanilla
- 1 ½ cups flour
- 2 tablespoons cocoa powder
- 1 teaspoon baking powder
- 1/2 cup chocolate chips

Nutritional Information

323 Calories
12.7g Fat
47.3g Carbs
2g Fiber
5.3g Protein

Directions

Add a metal trivet and 1 cup of water in your Instant Pot. Spray custard cups with a non-stick cooking spray. Set aside.

In a large bowl add the butter, sugar and eggs. Mix until smooth. Then stir in the milk, flour, cocoa powder and vanilla. Divide the mixture between the prepared custard cups.

Lower the cups onto the trivet.

Secure the lid. Choose the "Steam" mode and cook for 15 minutes at High pressure. When cooking is complete, use a natural pressure release for 5 minutes and carefully remove the lid.

Serve. Bon appetite!

Printed in Great Britain
by Amazon